READINGS ON EQUAL EDUCATION
(Formerly *Educating the Disadvantaged*)

READINGS ON EQUAL EDUCATION

Volume 18

EQUITY AND ACCESS IN HIGHER EDUCATION:
CHANGING THE DEFINITION OF EDUCATIONAL OPPORTUNITY

Volume Editor
M. Christopher Brown II

Managing Editor
Pamela S. Angelle

AMS PRESS, INC.
NEW YORK

READINGS ON EQUAL EDUCATION
VOLUME 18
Equity and Access in Higher Education:
Changing the Definition of Educational Opportunity

ISSN 0270-1448
Set ISBN 0-404-10100-3
Volume 18 ISBN 0-404-10118-6
Library of Congress Catalog Card Number 77-83137

All AMS Books are printed on acid-free paper that meets the guidelines for performance and durability of the Committee on Production Guidelines for Book Longevity of the Council on Library Resources.

AMS PRESS, INC.
BROOKLYN NAVY YARD, BLDG. 292, SUITE 417
63 FLUSHING AVENUE
BROOKLYN, NY 11205, USA

Manufactured in the United States of America

To my beloved grandmother
EVELYNA S. BROWN
at whose feet I first learned of
equity, opportunity, and education

CONTENTS

VOLUME 18

CONTRIBUTOR'S NOTES

F. KING ALEXANDER is President of Murray State University and former Assistant Professor and Director of the Higher Education Program at the University of Illinois at Urbana-Champaign. His research interests include state and federal financing of higher education and institutional revenue and expenditure patterns. His research also includes governmental assessments of institutional performance where he has worked on many state and federal projects.

PAMELA S. ANGELLE is the Effective Schools Coordinator for the Region IV Education Service Center of the Louisiana Department of Education. Her research interests focus on school effectiveness and school improvement, with an emphasis on the link between school effects and teacher effects on student achievement. Dr. Angelle served as Managing Editor of *Readings on Equal Education, Volume 17* and is also Managing Editor of this volume.

STEVEN R. ARAGON is an Assistant Professor in the Department of Human Resource Education at the University of Illinois at Urbana-Champaign. His research and teaching initiatives focus on teaching and learning issues of non-traditional students and students of color within community college settings. He is the recent editor of the New Directions for Community Colleges monograph, *Beyond Access: Methods and Models for Increasing Retention and Learning Among Minority Students* (2000). Dr. Aragon teaches courses in adult learning theory, program evaluation, and curriculum development.

M. CHRISTOPHER BROWN II is an Associate Professor of Education and Senior Research Associate in the Center for the Study of Higher Education at The Pennsylvania State University. His research investigates the systemic and structural challenges to effective and efficient functioning of postsecondary institutions and/or systems. This system of inquiry attempts to make visible the hidden voices of race and power in the law, policy, history, and governance surrounding and within colleges and universities. He is the author/editor of *The Quest to Define Collegiate Desegregation* (1999), *Organization and Governance in Higher Education*

(2000), and *Black Sons to Mothers* (2000, with James Earl Davis). He continues to conduct research on institutional climate, black colleges, and educational opportunity.

TIMOTHY K. EATMAN is a postdoctoral scholar at the Center for the Study of Higher and Postsecondary Education at the University of Michigan. Using a sociological theoretical orientation, his research examines the impact that institutional policies and programs have on student development with a particular focus on equity. In conjunction, his work examines the process by which students from groups that are traditionally underrepresented in higher education negotiate the transition between college and graduate degree programs.

ELIZABETH A. KEMPER is an Assistant Professor in the Department of Education Research, Leadership, and Counselor Education at North Carolina State University. Her research interests focus on school reform implementation and policy issues, specifically their impact upon economically disadvantaged students. She is currently the series coeditor of *Readings on Equal Education*, and most recently was a guest coeditor for an issue of the *Journal of Education for Students Placed At Risk* (2002, in press), investigating the impact of the Direct Instruction school reform model.

FRANKIE SANTOS LAANAN is Assistant Professor of Community College Leadership in the Department of Human Resource Education at the University of Illinois at Urbana-Champaign. He has published articles in journals such as *Research in Higher Education, Community College Review,* and *New Directions for Community Colleges.* He is coeditor of a *New Directions for Community Colleges* (Jossey-Bass) monograph titled, "Determining the Economic Benefit of Attending Community Colleges" (1998), and most recently, editor of a *New Directions for Community Colleges* monograph titled, "Transfer Students: Trends and Issues" (2001). His research focuses on student transition and the impact of postsecondary educational environments on student development, transition, and educational outcomes.

GLENDA DROOGSMA MUSOBA is a policy analyst at the Indiana Education Policy Center and is pursuing her doctorate in higher education at Indiana University. Her research interests include access and equity in college admissions, student persistence, and other justice issues in higher education.

KRISTINE K. OTTO is Assistant Director of Development in The Pennsylvania State University's College of Education. She earned a J.D. from the University of Connecticut School of Law prior to earning a Ph.D. in higher education from The Pennsylvania State University. Her research interests include affirmative action, desegregation, and nondiscrimination in higher education. Her doctoral dissertation was titled "Funding Underrepresented Minority Graduate Students: A Case Study with Legal Analysis."

HERALDO RICHARDS is an Associate Professor at Austin Peay State University in Clarksville, Tennessee. His research focuses on the instruction and evaluation of students with disabilities from culturally and linguistically diverse backgrounds.

JEANITA W. RICHARDSON is an Assistant Professor of Educational Policy in the School of Education and Allied Human Services at Hofstra University. Her completed and ongoing research investigates deterrents to health, distance education, and other educational access and equity issues. Each of her policy analyses examines social justice issues as they relate to the educational exchange and the disproportionate disadvantage they exact upon low status populations.

EDWARD P. ST. JOHN is a Professor in the Department of Educational Leadership and Policy Studies at Indiana University. His research on student financial aid and other postsecondary policy topics has appeared in *Research in Higher Education*, the *Journal of Higher Education*, the *Journal of Student Financial Aid* and other education research journals. His latest book is *Reinterpreting Urban School Reform: A Critical-Empirical Review* (coedited with Louis F. Miron), forthcoming from SUNY Press.

LINDA C. TILLMAN is an Associate Professor in the Department of Educational Leadership and Policy Studies at Wayne State University. Her research interests focus on mentoring African-American faculty, teachers and administrators, the education of

African-Americans in K-16 education, principalship preparation, and culturally responsive research approaches using qualitative methods. Recent publications include "Mentoring African-American Faculty in Predominantly White Institutions" in *Research in Higher Education.*

WILLIAM T. TRENT is Professor of Educational Policy Studies and Sociology at the University of Illinois at Urbana-Champaign. He recently completed serving five years as an Associate Chancellor at the University of Illinois and currently serves as co-chair of the Committee on Educational Excellence and Testing Equity, a National Academy of Science/National Research Council, Board on Testing and Assessment activity. Trent's research focuses on inequality and equity in education with a particular emphasis on school desegregation, access, desegregation in higher education and, most recently, equity issues in assessment. He is the principle investigator for a project examining the production of doctorate recipients among students of color.

EBONI M. ZAMANI is an Assistant Professor in higher education administration in the Department of Leadership and Counseling at Eastern Michigan University. Her research interests and publications have examined retention and transition among two- and four-year students, college readiness and remediation, and the changing context of attitudinal responses toward affirmative action in higher education.

INTRODUCTION

EQUITY AND ACCESS IN HIGHER EDUCATION: CHANGING THE DEFINITION OF EDUCATIONAL OPPORTUNITY

M. Christopher Brown II

The eighteenth volume of the series *Readings on Equal Education* focuses on issues of access and equity in postsecondary education. Although American higher education has always been diverse, the issue of equity and access to educational opportunity has been viewed from different vantages throughout its history. There exist historic pockets of inclusion across the panorama of postsecondary education (Brown, 1999). There are black colleges, tribal colleges, and colleges with a history of a large minority population; diversity programs and affirmative action initiatives; student exchanges and scholarship funds; federal legislation and court mandates; each intent on expanding educational opportunity. However, the scant academic literature regarding equity and access exude an ominous quiescence on the nexus to, with, and between educational opportunity. *Equity and Access in Higher Education: Changing the Definition of Educational Opportunity* fills a void in the literature regarding equity and access in postsecondary education. The readings are empirical, contextual, and useful.

The challenge that faces postsecondary education in the United States is marrying educational opportunity with educational outcomes. Until recently the typical campus population reflected the dominant racial, gender, sexual preference, ability, and economic composition of the nation. With the growing national discourse, there is a new focus on how college campuses can better reflect the multiple groups, languages, and perspectives of society. According to Rhoads (1995) "the emerging voices of multiculturalism highlight how higher education and the schooling process in general fundamentally is tied to issues of culture and identity" (p. 265).

Over the years many colleges and universities have taken the concept of educational opportunity seriously. These efforts to reform, revise, revamp, and remove the perennial preference for white, male, able-bodied, middle-class constituents has been fraught with opposition and legal challenges. Consequently, it is important to understand the competing views regarding these initiatives. More importantly, higher education writ large must acknowledge the effects of restricted educational opportunity on overall life success. There exists compelling evidence that bias and prejudice still persist in all phases of the higher education contin- uum (Brown & Land, forthcoming).

To date very little scholarly work has been proffered despite the proliferation of policy activity in the areas of equity and access. Given the changing face of American higher education, the time is ripe to reassess the policies, institutions, and issues which promote and delimit equity and access. This volume fulfills the need for careful investigation of the future prospects of equity and access in postsecondary education. This is an area of inquiry that is of increasing importance to national- and state-level policy makers, higher education officials, administrators, faculty, researchers, and the national citizenry. Like society writ large, education within the United States, too, must respond to the swelling population of students from myriad backgrounds and experiences. Consequently, the educational structure must also face the complex nuances of multiple cultures, languages, and contexts within the classroom, and within higher education on the college campus. At the postsecondary level, the multiplicity of these nuances requires particular attention as it relates to who gets into college and how well they perform academically.

Organization of This Volume

This volume is divided into two main parts, "The Collegiate Context" and "The Policy Context." Part I explores educational opportunity at the campus level, while Part II explores issues related to equity in terms of an overarching national perspective.

Part I begins with Laanan and Brown's cogent analysis of the changing college student population. The chapter contends that any discussion of postsecondary equity and access must be embedded in the data regarding who is affected and to what degree. Aragon and Zamani follow in chapter 2 by exploring the ways in which special population institutions have attempted to respond to the burgeoning populations within those student demographics. Alexander extends this discussion in chapter 3 with regard to his analysis of the ability of students to pay tuition and obtain financial aid.

The last two chapters in this section focus on institutional capacity. In chapter 4, Richardson contends that distance education has the capability to remove a number of barriers to educational opportunity. She notes that the ability to move barriers and the practice of moving barriers is not synonymous. Tillman's chapter 5, "Priming the Pump," investigates the nexus between faculty and student success. The basic argument is that institutions that have difficulty retaining diverse students also have difficulty retaining diverse faculty.

Part II of the volume employs a conceptual approach to the discussions of equity and access. Otto begins the section with a thorough examination of the legal context in which equity and access are being discussed in postsecondary settings. She details a legal backlash as it relates to educational opportunity. In chapter 7, St. John and Musoba reconceptualize the educational opportunity construct. Placing educational opportunity within the conversation initiated by Otto, they argue for a marriage between access and opportunity that has heretofore not been made.

The section continues with Trent and Eatman's analysis of race conscious programmatic initiatives in the educational opportunity paradigm. The contention is that race is a salient consideration; however, that its use must be monitored to avoid new forms of bias, errant assumptions, or both. The final chapter in this section by Richards focuses on student ability and Americans with Disabilities Act, and reminds the reader that diversity is not limited to issues of race, class, and gender.

Exploring Equity and Access

When one takes a critical look at the role that educational opportunity plays within higher education, it would be incomplete unless the notions of equity and access were concomitantly considered. Taking into account an individual's uniqueness as part of the admissions or programmatic criteria for persons in American colleges and universities has increasingly become a controversial practice. Should we treat people unequally in the pursuit of universal access? The answer is yes. On the issue of divorcing the notions of equality and equity, Gordon (1995) states:

> Care must be taken to make clear the difference between equity and equality. Equity speaks to and references fairness and social justice; it requires that the distribution of social resources be sufficient to the condition that is being treated. Equality, on the other hand, connotes sameness and the absence of discrimination. Rawls

eloquently reminds us that one of the fundamental tenets of social justice provides for an unequal distribution of social resources that favors the weaker members of the society. However, in societies that include unequal members, equal distribution may not be equitable. For example, if one person needs penicillin and the other needs tetracycline, and the hospital gives both penicillin, the two people have been treated equally, but it certainly cannot be claimed that they have been treated equitably. Or, if one person needs three doses and the other needs one dose of the same medicine, and both are given one dose, then they have been treated equally, but one has been deprived of what is sufficient to his or her needs, and thus has been treated inequitably. (pp. 363-364)

In order to provide the proper perspective to analyze this issue, we must first understand the circumstances that created the need for affirmative action and other equity programs. The American quest for equity began when Abraham Lincoln signed the Emancipation Proclamation and then enacted the passage of the Thirteenth Amendment (Brubacher & Rudy, 1997). Although the enslavement of diasporic Africans was outlawed, this did not mean that they were afforded the same rights and privileges as U.S. citizens of European descent. In fact, another century of "separate but equal" would pass before the Civil Rights movement could effectuate a national ethos of equity, access, and, most importantly, educational opportunity.

The quest for equity and access in postsecondary education is the continuing pursuit of a stratagem that both acknowledges and utilizes the sexually, racially, ethnically, politically, economically, physically, and linguistically diverse groups, along with the dominant majority in order to support and maintain diversity, tolerance, and, ultimately, community. The struggle over hegemony and power in student enrollment, staff employment, and curricular offerings will continue to loom large as long as groups within higher education seek to remain exclusive enclaves of superiority from which under-represented and marginalized groups must entreat special preferences and benevolent opportunities. Sacks (1997) notes that

the real challenge to higher education in America as we approach the millennium is how to come to terms with the fragmented and contested terrain of learning arising from profound shifts in mother culture itself. Once the public acknowledges this, reforming the system will be seen in a whole new light. (p. 80)

Together, the chapters in this book present a unique picture of the state of higher education in the United States. Although the year is now 2002, it is despite genuinely valiant efforts that we still live in a world where people are discriminated against and prejudice is rampant. This persistence of intentional restriction to access and blatant disregard for equity is posing a threat to the educational opportunity available to the myriad students and personnel involved in the higher education system. While the American system of postsecondary education has indeed come a long way, there remain many miles of uncharted territory to traverse. It is hoped that this volume presents a challenge to both critics and supporters of equity issues, inviting them to view this subject from a variety of perspectives.

References

Brown, M. C. (1999). *The quest to define collegiate desegregation: Black colleges, Title VI Compliance and Post-Adams Litigation.* Westport, CT: Bergin & Garvey.

Brown, M. C., & Land, R. R. (Eds.) (forthcoming, 2002). *The politics of curricular change: Essays on hegemony and power in education.* New York: Peter Lang.

Brubacher, J. S., & Rudy, W. (1997). *Higher education in transition: A history of American colleges and universities* 4th ed.). New Brunswick, NJ: Transaction.

Gordon, E. W. (1995). Toward an equitable system of educational assessment. *Journal of Negro Education, 64*(3), 360-372.

Rhoads, R. A. (1995). Critical multiculturalism, border knowledge, and the canon: Implications for general education and the academy. *The Journal of General Education, 44* (4), 256-273.

Sacks, P. (1997). Higher education at the end of the millennium. *Thought & Action, 13*(1), 69-80.

SECTION I.

The Collegiate Context

CHAPTER 1

PORTRAIT OF THE AMERICAN COLLEGE STUDENT: TRENDS AND ISSUES

Frankie Santos Laanan & M. Christopher Brown II

Introduction

Over a decade ago, Arthur Levine (1989) published a book that examined the projected demographic realities and changing opportunities of America's higher education for 1990-2000. This book provided a comprehensive picture of the student body of the 1990s, specifically, analyses of demographic trends of five key student populations (Black, Hispanic, and Asian minorities, traditional and non-traditional college-age students). In response to the groundbreaking work of Levine, there has been a wave of publications that continue to carry to the forefront the changing student demographics of American higher education.

For higher education researchers and scholars, the ability to present demographic statistics as well as to discuss emerging issues which face students in higher education continues to be an important area of scholarly interest. With the new millennium upon us, the higher education system of the United States is preparing to experience these changing student demographics. Not only are institutions faced with dealing with a more multicultural, multifaceted student body; but, institutions of higher learning are faced with the social, economic, political, and technological issues that make the changing of the student fabric ever so complex.

Between 1977 and 1987, enrollment in higher education increased by 13%. Additionally, between 1987 and 1997, enrollment increased at about the same rate, from 12.8 million to 14.3

million (U.S. Department of Education, 1999). The number of college eligible students seeking to pursue higher learning in the nation's two- and four-year colleges and universities is still rapidly expanding. According to the U.S. Department of Education, in the year 2010 projections are that college enrollment will increase to 17.4 million students (*The Chronicle of Higher Education*, 2000). Moreover, the number of minority individuals who reside in the United States is growing exponentially due to births and immigration, which, in turn, will impact enrollment in higher education institutions. With this growth of students, both from traditional and nontraditional backgrounds, American colleges and universities will be faced with numerous challenges over the next several decades. The projections suggest that the fabric of America's institutions of higher learning will change in different areas – constituents, access, participation, and progress. This chapter uses national data as a basis to provide a context and presents several issues that have emerged to the forefront including college choice, access and opportunity, and progress. Specifically, the purpose of the chapter is to address the following questions: What are the enrollment trends for the next decade? Who is the student body and from where are these students coming? How have the progress rates changed among and between racial/ethnic groups? And what are the implications of these data for higher education administrators, faculty, researchers and scholars, and policy makers?

This chapter is organized in two major sections. The first section presents different emerging issues that are discussed in academia, in political circles, and among students and other constituencies. The second section is devoted to addressing the questions that are posed in the beginning of this chapter. By using the numerous sources currently available, we attempt to synthesize and interpret the data by drawing conclusions regarding the critical issues facing the American college student.

Issues beyond the Horizon

What are the emerging issues including academic, social, political, economic, and technological that are being addressed in the new decade of the twenty-first century? What are the trends and statistics of the current and future enrollments of students in American higher education? What are the implications of a diverse student body and constituency with respect to higher education administrators, faculty, student affairs professionals, and the public? Finally, to what extent are students influenced in the context of a changing multicultural, highly technological, and competitive global economy in America? These are just some of the issues that this chapter will attempt to address. It is hoped that by presenting, discussing, and interpreting these issues in a synthesized fashion we will begin a dialogue on the perennial issues that will be among us for the next several decades.

College Choice

Currently, students have available the opportunity to pursue higher education in any one of the nation's 4,000 institutions of higher learning. According to the U.S. Department of Education (1999), post-secondary education includes an array of diverse educational experiences, including a wide range of programs offered by colleges and universities across the United States. Today more students than ever have a wide array of choice available to them. Students can attend a community college (or two-year institution) that offers vocational training or the first two-years of training at the college level; the highest degree from a two-year institution is an associate's degree (Cohen & Brawer, 1996). On the other hand, students can choose to attend a four-year college or university (public or private) which typically offers a full undergraduate course of study leading to a bachelor's degree as well as first-professional and graduate programs leading to advanced degrees. Other types of educational institutions include vocational and technical institutes that offer training programs designed to prepare students for specific careers. Other types of educational opportunities for adults are provided by community groups, religious organizations, libraries, and businesses (U.S. Department of Education, 1999).

In addition to the federal government's classification of post-secondary education institutions, the Carnegie Classification of Institutions of Higher Education has been a valuable framework. Developed in 1970 by the Carnegie Commission on Higher Education, the Carnegie Classification was used to aid its own policy research. The classification is considered the leading typology of American colleges and universities. Specifically, it is a framework in which institutional diversity in U.S. higher education is commonly described. The latest preliminary version (The

Carnegie Foundation for the Advance of Teaching, 2000), organizes institutions in six categories: doctorate-granting institutions (or research), master's (comprehensive) colleges and universities, baccalaureate colleges (e.g., liberal arts), associate's colleges, specialized institutions (e.g., theological seminaries and other specialized faith-related institutions; medical schools and medical centers; other health professional schools; schools of engineering and technology; schools of business and management; schools of art, music, and design), and tribal colleges and universities.

An important caveat made by the Carnegie Commission is that the typology or taxonomy is *not* a ranking of institutions, nor do its categories imply quality differences. The way an institution is assigned to a category is based on descriptive data about that institution. In general, the categories are intended to be relatively homogenous with respect to the institutions' functions as well as student and faculty characteristics. In 2005, the Carnegie Commission plans to issue a centennial edition with fundamental changes that may permit multiple classifications of institutions. According to the senior scholar involved in this process, the goal is to reorient the classification by 2005 to engage the foundation in fundamental thinking about how to characterize similarities and differences among institutions of higher education and how institutions and whole sets of institutions change.

The notion of college choice depends on various factors: institutional reputation and prestige, admissions standards, performance on standardized tests (i.e., SAT, ACT), institutional rankings, personal choice or preference, and economics. These are factors, which eventually lead an individual to pursue a particular college or university. Today, institutions of higher learning are competing to attract academically qualified students who represent diverse backgrounds to fill their spaces in their freshman classes. Because of the competitive market in higher education, admissions offices are faced with employing innovative marketing strategies to attract the student body of their choice. Moreover, students and parents are becoming smarter consumers and have available to them numerous educational avenues to pursue than decades before.

For many Americans choosing to attend a college or university means attending an institution that is deemed highly selective or prestigious. Selective institutions can either be publicly or privately controlled. Many of the nation's public universities (e.g.,

University of California at Berkeley, University of Illinois at Urbana-Champaign, University of Texas, etc.), which are the flagship institutions in their respective states are competing with Ivy League institutions for the best and brightest individuals. In the last few years, the *U.S. News and World Report* has published the annual rankings of colleges and universities. This publication has received attention from higher education administrators, faculty, students, parents, and other interested individuals. The controversy surrounding the college rankings is perpetuating certain values about a particular institution based on a set of criteria. According to *U.S. News*, the purpose of ranking colleges and universities is to help individuals (i.e., students and parents) make one of the most important decisions in terms of their educational investment. The magazine maintains that an investment in a college education could profoundly affect the career opportunities, financial well-being, and quality of life of individuals (*U.S. News and World Report*, 2000).

From the economic perspective, the issue of college choice also speaks to the resources available to the individuals. Obtaining admission to many of the nation's top colleges has become very competitive; as a result, some parents are relying on the expertise and assistance of private college counselors. This particular issue speaks to the disparity of an individual's economic or cultural capital. That is, only the individuals who are fortunate to have financial resources can utilize such resources. In the wake of an economic and financial boom, this raises fundamental questions about the "haves" and "have-nots," thus, separating the population into different social-economic status groups. For the growing number of ethnic minorities, especially the recent immigrants, such resources are virtually impossible.

Access and Opportunity
Access and opportunity have numerous meanings in the context of post-secondary education. Having access to education means having the freedom or ability to obtain or make use of resources and opportunities. In other words, given the size, scope, and comprehensiveness of the United States' post-secondary educational system, individuals have numerous options to pursue a variety of resource objectives depending on their academic or vocational interests. Opportunity, on the other hand, refers to the chance for advancement or progress. Astin (1982, 1985) has

written extensively on the concept of educational equity. Specifically, he maintains that educational equality can be understood by first deconstructing the terms: equal access and equal opportunity. According to Astin (1982, 1985), equal access refers to the idea that no person is denied entrance into an educational system due to race, gender, income, and social status. On the other hand, equal opportunity refers to the idea that no person is denied the benefits of the education system because of race, gender, income, and social status. These concepts are often discussed in higher education literature in terms of their socio-political aspects.

An important question that continues to be raised is whether an individual can truly have equal access and equal opportunity in higher education? Answering this question can lead to a debate as to how one defines the terms and interprets the concepts. However, as Astin (1982, 1985) points out, everyone can have equal opportunity; however, not everyone can have equal access to institutions of higher learning. An example of this would be the rigorous and competitive admission requirements of most highly selective institutions. Highly selective institutions usually have internationally renowned reputations and highly selective requirements; they are often deemed by the general public to be prestigious colleges and universities. Therefore, students who do not have the credentials to meet these entrance requirements are not likely to have access to such institutions.

Although the traditional route to a four-year college or university college is straight after high school graduation, today there are many avenues an individual can pursue to attend an institution of choice, whether it is an Ivy League institution, a selective public research university, prestigious liberal arts college, or any other post-secondary institution. In states like California where there is a Master Plan for Higher Education, individuals can begin their post-secondary education at a public community college and complete the first two years of general education and then transfer to one of the 23 California State Universities or nine University of California campuses. Although an individual is not guaranteed acceptance, the formalized articulation of course requirements is state-mandated, and therefore, provides eased entry for prospective students transfer to a four-year college or university. Other states that have developed their own state systems that mirror California's three-tiered system include Illinois, Pennsylvania, and Kentucky.

It is impossible to talk about access and opportunity without addressing the contributions of the American community colleges, nontraditional universities, and the role of distance education. Each plays a unique role in American higher education and serves a diverse student population. For many minorities, the community college is viewed as the primary institution of choice (Phillippe, 2000). In fact, almost half of all undergraduates in higher education attend a community college. With over 10 million credit and non-credit students, the American community colleges play an integral role in providing educational access and opportunity to a diverse constituency. Today there are more than 1,000 public and private community colleges, at least one in every state. A uniquely American tradition, community colleges provide a variety of programs and fields of study for a diverse student population. Students who enroll in community colleges are anything but typical, in that they tend to be from all ages, ethnic groups, and backgrounds. With an emphasis on open access admission and accessibility, community colleges enroll almost half of all ethnic minority students in higher education. In fact, more than 50% of students with a disability are enrolled in a community college and nearly two-thirds of students are older than the traditional age of 21, and the number of students aged 40 or older is projected to increase significantly in the next few decades (Phillippe, 2000).

Although to most Americans the college-going experience might mean moving away from home and living in campus housing, there is a new phenomenon that has received attention. The University of Phoenix, which was founded in 1976, is considered to be the nation's largest private accredited university. With an enrollment of over 75,000 degree-seeking students, the University of Phoenix provides educational opportunities to working adults at more than 92 campuses and learning centers in 15 states, Puerto Rico and Canada, and around the world via the Internet. This phenomenon has transformed America's higher education in terms of access, equity, and opportunity. To date, more than 93,000 students have earned their degree from one of the University of Phoenix campuses. In 1989, University of Phoenix became one of the first accredited colleges to provide online degree programs. The university prides itself on a faculty of over 7,000 members who hold masters and doctoral degrees in numerous fields. Given the philosophy of the university, the faculty hold high-level positions within the fields they teach, and have an average of 15 years of work experience. The average student age is 35 and over 75% of students receive some form of tuition reimbursement from their employers (University of Phoenix, www.phoenix.edu/students/index.html).

Another phenomenon in higher education is distance education. According to the National Center for Education Statistics (NCES), distance education is emerging as an increasingly important component of higher education (1998). In a study conducted in 1995, NCES surveyed 50 states, the District of Columbia, and Puerto Rico. Table 1 presents the distribution of higher education institutions that currently, or plan to use distance education. The table presents data for all institutions, institutional type (i.e., public and private two- and four-year), geographic region, and enrollment.

The results of the study indicated that over one-third (or 33%) of all institutions offered distance education courses, 25% planned to begin offering distance education courses in the next three years, and 42% indicated no plans to offer distance education courses in the next three years. Interestingly, 62% of public four-year and 58% two-year institutions currently offer distance education. Conversely, a small percentage of private two- and four-year institutions currently offer distance education. Slightly more than one-third of the West, Central and Southeast regions currently offer distance education. However, less than one-fourth (or 20%) of institutions from the Northeast offer distance education.

The findings from this survey have several implications. First, given that public institutions are likely to enroll a substantially larger student population, students are given nontraditional avenues to complete course work. Second, it is evident that institutions from the Northeast are less likely to offer distance education for their students. This finding suggests several things: there are likely to be more private institutions in this region and students are likely to be of traditional background.

Table 1. Percentage Distribution of Higher Education Institutions, by Current and Planned Use of Distance Education: 1995.

Institutional Characteristics	Currently offer distance education	Plan to offer distance educ. in next 3 yrs	No plans to offer distance educ. in next 3 yrs
Institutional Types			
Public: 2 yr.	58	28	14
Private: 2 yr.	2	14	84
Public: 4 yr.	62	23	14
Private: 4 yr.	12	27	61
Geographic Region			
Northeast	20	27	53
Southeast	31	28	41
Central	39	24	37
West	40	23	37
Enrollment			
Less than 3000	16	27	56
3,000 to 9,999	61	24	15
10,000 or more	76	14	10

Note: Data are for higher education institutions in the 50 states, the District of Columbia, and Puerto Rico. Percents may not sum to 100 because of rounding. Source: U.S. Department of Education, N.C.E.S., Post-secondary Education Quick Information System, Survey on Distance Education Courses Offered by Higher Education Institutions, 1995.

Progress

With the advent of distance education, teaching and learning has taken on new meaning in higher education. For students, the Internet can serve as a medium to enroll in a particular course and/or program and learn from the comfort of their homes. Referred to as online courses, many colleges and universities are offering courses via the Internet. As mentioned earlier, the University of Phoenix is a prime example of an institution that prides itself in offering high-quality education to a diverse student population. From undergraduate to graduate students, the University of Phoenix is dedicated to meet the educational needs of working professionals and their employers. Another segment of higher education that utilizes distance education are community colleges. For decades, community colleges have channeled efforts to offer educational programs to a diverse constituency by employing technology such as distance education or online courses. In fact, community colleges continue to provide access to education to anyone who wants it (Cohen & Brawer, 1996).

Although technology is a critical element in today's society in the workplace or in the educational environment, the extent to which it impacts student development, learning, and satisfaction continues to raise important questions for researchers. With the growing number of distance online courses being offered today, the numbers are expected to rise in the coming decades. Not only are students involved in the process, the role of faculty in terms of teaching and learning brings new meaning to delivering instruction. For the growing number of students who are taking distance courses via the Internet, the role of student services and learning community takes on new meanings. These changes have implications for students, faculty, and other college personnel. The human interaction that is not available in online courses continues to be a hot topic among researchers and scholars in education and other disciplines.

Past, Present and Future Enrollment Trends

According to the U.S. Department of Education (1999), the number of older students has been growing more rapidly than the number of younger students, but this pattern is beginning to change. Between 1990 and 1997, the enrollment of students under 25 increased by 2%. During the same period, enrollment of persons 25 and over rose by 6%. From 1997 to 2000, NCES projects a rise of 6% in enrollments of persons under 25 and an increase of 3% in the number of 25 and over. In terms of enrollment, the trends have differed at the undergraduate, graduate, and first-professional levels. Undergraduate enrollment increased during the 1970s, but dipped slightly between 1983 and 1985. From 1985 to 1992, undergraduate enrollment increased each year, rising 18% before declining slightly and stabilizing between 1993 and 1997. For graduate enrollments, the number has been consistent at about 1.3 million in the late 1970s and early 1980s, but rose 27% between 1985 and 1997. After rising very rapidly during the 1970s, enrollment in first-professional programs stabilized in the 1980s. There was an 8% increase in first-professional enrollment between 1985 and 1997.

The proportion of American students in higher education who are minorities has been increasing (Levine & Cureton, 1998). In 1976, 16% were minorities, compared with 27% in 1997. Much of the change can be attributed to rising numbers of Hispanics and Asian students. The proportion of Asian and Pacific Islander students rose from 2% to 6%, and the Hispanic proportion rose from 4% to 9% during that time period. The proportion of black students fluctuated during most of the early part of the period, before rising slightly to 11% in 1997.

Table 2 presents statistical data of the total college enrollment by racial and ethnic groups for selected years. The table includes data for American Indian, Asian, Black, Hispanic, White, and foreign students for selected years from 1976 to 1997 (U.S. Department of Education). The data presented for 1996 and 1997 are not directly comparable with those of previous years because of a change in the way the U.S. Department of Education categorizes colleges and universities. Until 1996, enrollment data covered institutions accredited at the post-secondary level by an agency recognized by the department. Starting in 1996, the data cover degree-granting institutions eligible to participate in federal Title IV programs. The two classification systems are similar; the new one includes some additional, primarily two-year colleges, and excludes a few colleges that did not award degrees.

Overall, the total number of students enrolled in the nation's colleges and universities grew from 10.9 million in 1976 to 14.5 million in 1997. For all groups, the college enrollment increased during the specific years reported. Specifically, among Black and White students, the enrollment pattern has increased in a steady pace. However, among Asians and Hispanics, the growth from 1980 to 1997 is substantial. The college enrollment almost triples for both groups. A possible attribution is the growth of immigrant populations to the United States in the last few decades. Further, college education is perceived by these groups as a mechanism to upward social, economic, and political mobility.

Table 2. Total College Enrollment by Racial and Ethnic Group, Selected Years.

Group	1976	1980	1990	1995	1996	1997
Amer. Indian	76,100	83,900	102,800	131,300	137,600	142,500
Asian	197,900	286,400	572,400	797,400	828,200	859,200
Black	1,033,000	1,106,800	1,247,000	1,473,700	1,505,600	1,551,000
Hispanic	383,000	471,700	728,400	1,093,800	1,166,100	1,218,500
White	9,076,100	9,833,000	10,722,500	10,311,200	10,263,900	10,266,100
Foreign	218,700	305,000	391,500	454,400	466,300	465,000
All	10,985,600	12,086,800	13,818,600	14,261,800	14,367,500	14,502,300

Source: U.S. Department of Education, 1997.   Note: Because of rounding, details may not add to totals.

Table 3 presents projections of college enrollment by institutional control, enrollment status, and gender for selected years. The information includes data in two-year increments from 2000-2010. Currently, the total college enrollment is over 15 million students. This number is expected to increase to 17.4 million by 2010. Over three-fourths of these students are enrolled in public colleges and universities. The number of college students enrolled in public post-secondary institution is expected to increase from 11.7 million in 2000 to 13.6 million. Conversely, the growth at private institutions will more than likely increase, but not to the magnitude of public institutions.

Table 3. Projections of College Enrollment Status and Gender.

	2000	2002	2004	2006	2008	2010
Institutional Control						
Total	15,135,000	15,500,000	15,874,000	16,336,000	16,975,000	17,490,000
Public	11,795,000	12,080,000	12,370,000	12,726,000	13,216,000	13,607,000
Private	3,340,000	3,420,000	3,505,000	3,610,000	3,759,000	3,882,000
Enrollment Status						
Full time	8,665,000	8,888,000	9,130,000	9,432,000	9,912,000	10,313,000
Part time	6,470,000	3,613,000	6,745,000	6,904,000	7,063,000	7,176,000
Men						
Total	6,481,000	6,614,000	6,749,000	6,900,000	7,126,000	7,320,000
Full time	3,917,000	3,998,000	4,080,000	4,167,000	4,328,000	4,474,000
Part time	2,563,000	2,616,000	2,670,000	2,732,000	2,798,000	2,847,000
Women						
Total	8,655,000	8,886,000	9,125,000	9,437,000	9,849,000	10,169,000
Full time	4,748,000	4,890,000	5,050,000	5,265,000	5,584,000	5,840,000
Part time	3,906,000	3,997,000	4,075,000	4,172,000	4,265,000	4,330,000

Source: U.S. Department of Education, 1997. Note: The table shows the "middle-alternative forecast," which represents the most likely outcome. Details may not add to totals because of rounding.

Among full-time students, the growth of college enrollments is expected to be from 8.6 million in 2000 to over 10.3 million by 2010. The number of women enrolled in post-secondary education is expected to increase at higher rates than men. By 2010, women will comprise over 10.1 million students compared to 7.3 million of men. Interestingly, the growth of women attending college part-time is expected to surpass the rates of men over the next decade.

Where Do Students Come From?

According to the U.S. Department of Education (1997), there were over 9.2 million students enrolled in the nation's four-year colleges and universities, compared to 5.8 in two-year institutions. By 2010 the number of students enrolled in the nation's post-secondary education institutions is expected to increase from 9.2 million to over 10.8 million. However, for two-year colleges, the size and scope of noncredit students (i.e., students enrolled in courses that do not award credits) equal the amount of credit students, which today is estimated at 10 million. Although Table 4 indicates a sizeable increase in the next ten years, this number does not include noncredit figures. According to the American Association of Community Colleges, there is inconsistent data collection for non-credit students (Phillippe, 2000). AACC estimates that more than 5 million students each year participate in some form of non-credit activity at a community college. Non-credit courses are diverse and include a variety of educational objectives such as career, technical, vocational, and personal interest. It is estimated that many colleges around the country offer non-credit courses that lead to vendor certification (e.g., computer training, automotive competency, managerial enrich-ment). Further, colleges offer noncredit courses to local business and industry, government agencies, and other organizations.

Table 4.   Projections of College Enrollment by Institutional Type, Selected Years.

	2000	2002	2004	2006	2008	2010
4-Year						
Total	9,288,000	9,519,000	9,756,000	10,050,000	10,466,000	10,814,000
Public	6,157,000	6,313,000	6,471,000	6,667,000	6,944,000	7,176,000
Private	3,131,000	3,206,000	3,285,000	3,384,000	3,523,000	3,638,000
2-Year						
Total	5,847,000	5,981,000	6,119,000	6,286,000	6,509,000	6,675,000
Public	5,638,000	5,767,000	5,899,000	6,060,000	6,272,000	6,431,000
Private	209,000	214,000	220,000	226,000	237,000	244,000

Source: U.S. Department of Education, 1997.
Note: The table shows the "middle-alternative forecast," which represents the most likely outcome. Details may not add to totals because of rounding.

In the next few decades, the growth of first-generation students and ethnic minorities is expected to increase substantially. Moreover, students attending private post-secondary institutions such as the University of Phoenix will grow exponentially in the next decade. Finally, with the growth of distance of education, many more students will have access to higher education than ever before.

Statistical information at the national level in four areas – high school completion, college participation and educational attainment, college graduation rates, and degrees conferred – detail the matriculation pattern of college students (U.S. Department of Education, 1999). The information presents a portrait at the national level. Further, because of the growing number of minority students (i.e., African Americans, Hispanics, Asian Americans, and American Indians) in higher education, data are also reported by racial/ethnic background.

The National Picture

During the 1997-98 academic year, 4,064 accredited institutions offered degrees at the associate degree level or above. These included 2,309 four-year colleges and universities, and 1,755 two-year colleges. Institutions awarding various higher education degrees in 1996-97 numbered 2,470 for associate degrees, 1,868 for bachelor's, 1,391 for master's degrees, and 504 for doctor's degrees. The following is a breakdown of the latest data available by the U.S. Department of Education (1999):

- Between 1986-87 and 1996-97, the number of associate, bachelors', masters', and doctors' degrees rose.
- Associate degrees increased 31%, bachelors' degrees increased 18%, masters' degrees increased 45%, and doctors' degrees increased 35% during this period.
- The total number of bachelors' degrees increased slowly during the early 1980s and more rapidly towards the end of that decade, especially for women.
- Between 1986-87 and 1996-97, the number of bachelors' degrees awarded to men increased by 8%, while those awarded to women rose by 28%.

- Of the 1,173,000 bachelor's degrees conferred in 1996-97, the largest numbers of degrees were conferred in business (227,000), social sciences (125,000), and education (105,000).
- At the masters' degree level, the largest fields were education (110,000) and business (98,000). The largest fields at the doctoral level were education (6,800), engineering (6,200), biological and life science (4,800) and physical sciences (4,500)

According to the U.S. Department of Education, more people are completing education. Obtaining an education beyond high school is essential to secure a bright economic future. Researchers note that there is a positive relationship between education and earnings (Sanchez & Laanan, 1998). That is, the more education completed, the higher the earnings an individual is expected to gain in the world of work.

The next section provides a synopsis of statistical information from minority groups in post-secondary education. The information and data derive from publications from the U.S. Department of Education (1999) and the American Council's on Education (2000) annual status report of *Minorities in Higher Education.*

High School Completion

For many Americans, completing high school is an important step to making progress in the educational pipeline. Upon completing high school, students either choose to pursue employment and/or continue their education. In 1997 the high school completion rates for White, African Americans, and Hispanics differed significantly (U.S. Department of Commerce, 1998). Among 18- to 24-year-olds, White students had a graduation completion rate of 82.7%, compared to 74.7% of African Americans and 62.0% of Hispanics. Of these three groups, 67.7% of White, 60% of African American, and 54.3% of Hispanic students enrolled in college for one or more years. In terms of the population currently enrolled in college, Whites had higher rates (45.3%) of graduation, compared to 39.8% of African Americans and 36% of Hispanics. Clearly, the statistics show the different patterns of high school completion and college enrollment.

College Participation and Educational Attainment

From 1977 to 1997 the percentage of high school graduates currently enrolled in college increased from 32.5% to 45.2%. Similarly, the percentage of 18- to 24-year-olds currently enrolled during the same period rose from 26.1% to 36.9% (U.S. Department of Commerce, 1998). For African Americans, their college-going rates improved considerably during the 1990s due to gains made by women. In 1997, African Americans had the largest gender gap in college participation rates of the three major ethnic groups. Among the Hispanic population, their college participation rates for high school graduates ages 18 to 24 increased by only one percentage point, to 36%, in 1997. However, since 1990, Hispanics' college-going rate has increased nearly 8 percentage points. For men, the college participation rate increased from 30.2% in 1996 to 32.5% in 1997. However, for Hispanic women, the corresponding rate remained unchanged (39.6% and 39.7%, respectively).

College Graduation Rates

Although enrolling in college does not guarantee completion, there are many factors that can facilitate or impede an individual's successful completion. Both internal and external factors can play a role in possibly explaining the eventual college completion of students. The literature is filled with numerous research findings that help to explain possible reasons for not completing college (Astin, 1982, 1985; Pascarella & Terenzini, 1991). For African American, Hispanic, Asian American, American Indian, and White students who were freshmen in 1991-92, a study was conducted by the National Collegiate Athletic Association (1998) to analyze the six-year college graduation rates of students at NCAA Division I institutions. Nationwide, students at Division I institutions in 1997 posted a six-year graduation rate of 56%. When the data are disaggregated by racial/ethnic group, the highest graduation completion rates were among Asian Americans (65%), followed by Whites (58%), Hispanics (45%), African Americans (40%), and American Indians (36%).

Degrees Conferred by Racial/Ethnic Background

According to the American Council on Education (2000), students of color have earned increasing numbers of degrees since the 1980s. Although the rate of growth has varied considerably among the four major ethnic groups, they have made gains as a group at every degree level. Based on ACE's report, minority students have outpaced white students in their rate of increase at all degree levels since 1987. In fact, the proportion of bachelor's degrees awarded to students of color increased from 12.1% in 1987 to 19.8% in 1997. During the same period, the percentage of first-professional degrees awarded to minorities increased from 11.2% to 21%. Although these statistics appear to be in an upswing for minority students, compared to their enrollments, students of color remain under-represented at every degree level.

In terms of minority students' share of enrollments (U.S. Department of Education, 1999), the largest enrollments among students of color are in two-year institutions (31.3%), followed by four-year undergraduate enrollments (24%), professional school enrollments (23.4%), and graduate enrollments (17.1%). In terms of degrees conferred, the minority students' posted the highest degree completion of associate degrees (22.8%), followed by first-professional (21.0%), bachelor's (19.8%), master's (15.4%), and doctorates (8.4%).

Conclusion

The statistics and projections provided in this chapter paint an important picture of the emerging issues regarding the student body in two- and four-year colleges and universities in the United States. The role of colleges and universities is to provide quality education to a diverse student population. Specifically, with the growing number of students of color in post-secondary education, arguably there are benefits of racial and diversity in higher education (Milem & Hakuta, 2000). Milem & Hakuta (2000) eloquently articulate the reasons racial and ethnic diversity should be an important factor in admissions and hiring practices. Specifically, they maintain that the benefits of diversity are four-fold:

- racial and ethnic diversity enriches the educational experience;
- racial and ethnic diversity promotes personal growth and a healthy society;
- racial and ethnic diversity strengthens communities and the workplace; and

• racial and ethnic diversity enhances America's economic competitiveness.

There are numerous implications for higher education administrators, researchers and scholars, policy makers, students, and various constituencies. For administrators, the challenge for the twenty-first century is to balance racial and ethnic diversity and competition with respect to recruitment and admission of students, hiring of faculty, and resources to ensure the success of all students. From a research perspective, scholars are urged to rethink the ways in which research is undertaken. That is, employing innovative research strategies using multi-disciplinary frameworks will enhance our understanding of all students. Further, students will continue to pursue alternative educational opportunities depending on their educational goal, interest, or desire. These are complex issues that will be upon us for the next decade. Education is about furthering one's knowledge and expanding the intellectual and personal capacities of faculty, students, and the public. The challenge before us is to create environments – learning, community, technological, and socially responsive spaces for students, faculty, and the general public. The statistics show that the demographics will change and the fabric of the American colleges and universities will be transformed with the social, political and economic tides.

Higher education must pay greater attention to the where, how, and why students enter systems or sites of post-secondary education. The demand for an educated citizenry and workforce has never been greater. As society acknowledges the role and place of everyone in the global economy, the challenge of defining the college student will be critical to ongoing and developing efforts aimed at educational access, opportunity, and attainment. The ability of higher education to recognize the increasingly diverse composition of the college classroom will affect higher education for years to come.

References

American Council on Education (ACE) and American Association of University Professors (AAUP). (2000). Does Diversity Make a Difference? Three Research Studies on Diversity in College Classroom? Washington, D.C.: ACE and AAUP. (Internet reference: www.acenet.edu, or www.aaup.org).

American Council on Education. Minorities in Higher Education 1999-2000. Seventeenth Annual Status Report. Washington, D.C.: American Council on Education.

Astin, A. W. (1982). *Minorities in American Higher Education: Summary of Findings.* San Francisco: Jossey-Bass Publishers.

Astin, A. W. (1985). *Achieving Educational Excellence.* San Francisco: Jossey-Bass Publishers.

Carnegie Foundation for the Advancement of Teaching, The. (2000). *Carnegie Commission of Institutions of Higher Education, 2000 Edition.* Menlo Park, CA: The Carnegie Foundation for the Advancement of Teaching.

Chronicle of Higher Education Almanac Issue, The: 2000-2001. Volume XLVII, Number 1. Washington, D.C.: The Chronicle of Higher Education.

Cohen, A. M., & Brawer, F. B. (1996). *The American Community College.* (3rd Edition). San Francisco: Jossey-Bass Publishers.

Cohen, A. M. (1998). *The Shaping of American Higher Education: Emergence and Growth of the Contemporary* System. San Francisco: Jossey-Bass Publishers.

Levine, A. (1989). *Shaping of Higher Education's Future: Demographic Realities and Opportunities, 1990-2000.* San Francisco: Jossey-Bass Publishers.

Levine, A., & Cureton, J. S. (1998). *When Hope and Fear Collide: A Portrait of Today's Student.* San Francisco: Jossey-Bass Publishers.

Milem, J. F., & Hakuta, K. (2000). The Benefits of Racial and Ethnic Diversity in Higher Education. In *Minorities in Higher Education: 1999-2000.* Seventeenth Annual Status Report. Washington, D.C.: American Council on Education.

National Center for Education Statistics (1995). *Survey on Distance Education Offered by Higher Education Institutions.* Washington, D.C.: U.S. Department of Education.

National Center for Education Statistics (February 1998). Distance Education in Higher Education Institutions: Incidence, Audiences, and Plans to Expand. Issue Brief. Washington, D.C.: U.S. Department of Education, Office of Educational Research and Improvement.

National Collegiate Athletic Association (1998). *Division I Graduation Rates Report*. Indianapolis, IN: National Collegiate Athletic Association.

Pascarella, E. T., & Terenzini, P. T. (1991). *How College Affects Students: Findings and Insights of Twenty Years of Research*. San Francisco: Jossey-Bass Publishers.

Phillippe, K. A. (ed.) (2000). *National Profile of Community Colleges: Trends & Statistics, 3rd Edition*. Washington, D.C. Community College Press.

Sanchez, J. R., & Laanan, F. S. (eds.) (1998). Determining the Economic Benefits of Attending Community Colleges. *New Directions for Community Colleges*, Volume 104. San Francisco: Jossey-Bass Publishers.

University of Phoenix. About the University of Phoenix. http://www.phoenix.edu/students/index.html

Upcraft, M. L., Schuh, J. H. (1996). *Assessment in Student Affairs: A Guide for Practitioners*. San Francisco: Jossey-Bass Publishers.

U.S. Department of Commerce. (1998). School Enrollment – Social and Economic Characteristics of Students: October 1997. Current Population Reports, P-20 Series. Washington, D.C.: U.S. Department of Commerce, Bureau of the Census.

U.S. Department of Education. (1999). *Digest of Education Statistics*. Washington, D.C.: U.S. Department of Education, National Center for Education Statistics.

U.S. News and World Report. (2000). Why U.S. News Ranks Colleges. (www.usnews.com/usnews/edu/college/rankings/primer.htm).

CHAPTER 2

PROMOTING ACCESS AND EQUITY THROUGH MINORITY-SERVING AND WOMEN'S INSTITUTIONS

Steven R. Aragon & Eboni M. Zamani

Introduction

During the last decade, minority-serving and women's institutions in the United States have experienced a resurgence in both enrollment and prominence. As recently as the early 1980s, these schools – particularly historically Black colleges and universities – experienced stagnant and even declining enrollment as well as a general loss of visibility as providers of educational opportunity for underserved populations. Today, minority-serving and women's colleges and universities are a major component in the postsecondary education of minority and female students.

In many ways, the newfound stature of minority-serving institutions should come as no surprise. The nonwhite population of the United States, and of American higher education, is growing at record rates. As a result of this growth, the higher education establishment and nonminority institutions have been challenged to pay increased attention to this evolving group of schools. What is surprising about this resurgence, however, is that little of the growth has been the result of coordinated efforts on the part of these institutions to work together and seek common goals (Merisotis & O'Brien, 1998). In a range of arenas, most noticeably in federal government support for developing institutions, minority-serving institutions are in competition for limited resources. Yet despite this competitive pressure, minority-serving institutions have

23

prospered, not only in terms of student enrollments but also in political recognition and in the success of the students they educate.

This chapter is intended to serve as a primer on the growing group of minority-serving institutions, with the goal of educating leaders at mainstream institutions, analysts, and the minority-serving institutions themselves about the distinct purposes and common goals of these institutions. An increased understanding of minority-serving institutions and of their roles in educating underserved populations is important as the nation's demographic profile becomes increasingly diverse.

Minority-serving institutions are defined in this chapter primarily as those colleges and universities that are designated as historically Black colleges and universities (HBCUs), tribal colleges, Hispanic-serving institutions (HSIs) and women's colleges. These designations have been accorded through various federal policies and programs designed to encourage the development and growth of the institutions. As this chapter points out, the history, purposes, and operating structures of these institutions vary considerably. Yet despite their differences, minority-serving institutions share many goals related to educating underserved populations. These common goals make it important to understand the shared visions and missions of these institutions, and candidly to air their unique roles and concerns as they build for the future.

Background

Although the last four decades have brought improved social status and access to education for ethnic minorities, African Americans, Hispanics, Asians/Pacific Islanders, and American Indians/Alaska Natives are still disenfranchised (Aragon, 2000). According to researchers, minority students are more likely than their White counterparts to be at risk of academic failure at the elementary, secondary, and postsecondary levels (O'Brien & Zudak, 1998; Rendon & Hope, 1996). The risk factors associated with not completing a postsecondary program include delayed enrollment, part-time attendance, being self-supporting, single-parent status, full-time work schedules, caring for a dependent, and holding a GED certificate. According to a National Postsecondary Student Aid Study (as reported by O'Brien & Zudak, 1998), 27% of Hispanic students, 31% of African American students, and 35%

of American Indian/Alaska Native students have four or more of these risk factors, compared with 22% of White students. Another potential risk for minority students is that they often break new ground as the first in their families to attend college. While these data represent the averages for the different groups of students, enormous diversity exists within these four populations.

Today, racial and ethnic minorities make up about 28% of the U.S. population (U.S. Bureau of the Census, 1998). According to the U.S. Bureau of the Census (1996a) projections, by 2050 minorities will make up about 47% of the U.S. population. The implications of neglecting to better understand and address the learning needs of people of color for society, in general, and adult education, in particular, are staggering. Briscoe and Ross (1989) note that

> it is likely that young people will leave school early, will never participate fully in society or in the decision-making processes of government, and that they will neither enjoy the benefits of good health, nor experience the upward mobility needed as adults to make them full contributors and partners in shaping and participating in the larger society. (p. 586)

A decade later, these issues have yet to be resolved (O'Brien & Zudak, 1998; Rendon & Hope, 1996).

Today's Demographics
Students of color account for almost one-quarter (24.8%) of postsecondary education enrollment, with African Americans representing approximately 12%, Hispanics 9%, Asians/Pacific Islanders 3 %, and American Indians/Alaska Natives .8 % (O'Brien & Zudak, 1998). During the period between 1988 and 1997, enrollment of minority students across all institutions of higher education had a change of 57.2%, while White (non-Hispanic) enrollment saw a negative 0.2% change (American Council on Education, 2000). As a result of these demographic changes within society at large and institutions of higher education specifically, the term minority is losing its statistical meaning, as a new student majority rapidly emerges, comprising, collectively, African Americans, Hispanics/Latinos, Asians/Pacific Islanders, and American Indians/Alaska Natives (Rendon & Hope, 1996).

It is important, however, to keep in mind that within American higher education, community colleges play a significant role in providing educational access and opportunity to minority students. Each fall, approximately half of all minority undergraduates enrolled in higher education attend a community college. Arguably, community college campuses reflect the diversity of the American population. Enrolled students are of all ages and from different cultural and ethnic backgrounds. In fact, among minorities, community colleges are typically the schools of choice (American Association of Community Colleges, 1998).

According to the American Association of Community Colleges, these institutions saw an increase in enrollments of minority students between 1992 and 1997 (American Association of Community Colleges, 2000). The American Council on Education (2000) reports a 56.1% change in the enrollment of minority students in four-year institutions between 1988 and 1997. The community college saw a slightly higher percentage change (58.5%) in the enrollment of minority students during this same period.

Environment: The Influence of Institutional Type and Mission
The institutional mission reflects the intentions and direction of a college that involves establishing a statement of purpose that will endure and distinguishes types of institutions (Peeke, 1994). Community college missions have a uniqueness that sets them apart from senior institutions with regard to more than just the highest degree conferred. Referred to as the "people's colleges," two-year institutions were designed to extend higher education opportunities through a system of open admissions that has aided numerous first-generation, underprepared, financially wrought, and underrepresented college-bound students (Cohen & Brawer, 1996; Richardson & Skinner, 1992). However, within the two-year sector are institutions with dual missions, 1) open door admittance; and 2) serving a specific marginalized group. Because many American educational institutions did not voluntarily seek diversity among its participants, special focus colleges emerged (Townsend, 1999). Hence, minority-serving, two- and four-year institutions originated out of efforts to assist in navigating the terrain of racial tensions and gender disparities within education as well as within a larger societal context.

Community colleges provide routes to baccalaureate degrees by filling existing gaps in educational access for those who may not have other options for postsecondary attendance. Baccalaureate aspirants entering two-year colleges often differ from students attending four-year colleges or universities with regard to precollegiate preparation (Dougherty, 1987; Richardson & Bender, 1987). Thus, the role of admissions and enrollment in two- and four-year institutions of higher education varies due to divergent settings (Adelman, 1999).

Community colleges have a unique purpose, yet are still similar to four-year institutions. In addressing the varying missions, functions, students, and curricula of community colleges, Katsinas (1993) developed a community college classification system comprised of fourteen distinct types. The various types of community colleges include:

- institutions with comprehensive offerings located in rural areas;
- suburban colleges with an emphasis on liberal arts and transfer;
- urban/inner city colleges with a focus on vocational courses and school-to-work;
- metropolitan college districts with centralized and decentralized governance;
- colleges in close proximity to residential universities;
- mixture of the above categories;
- predominately Hispanic-serving institutions;
- historically Black two-year colleges;
- tribal community colleges;
- colleges devoted only to general education and transfer;
- exclusively technical colleges;
- non-profit private institutions (sectarian and non-sectarian);
- private proprietary colleges;
- community colleges administered directly by four-year institutions.

Institutional type and mission largely influence campus environments, and are important factors in students actualizing the aspirations to earn baccalaureate degrees. Among recipients of community college degrees, larger numbers of women receive associate degrees and certificates while a greater number of White students in general are awarded two-year degrees and certificates. Although roughly 25% of two-year collegians intend to obtain a certificate or associate degree without aspirations for the baccalaureate or beyond, many others intend to transfer to senior institutions. In underscoring the desire for higher degrees within the United States, one-fifth of the population has attained a bachelor's degree or higher.

Still, institutions also vary in accordance with how they are controlled. Privately controlled institutions foster student development, retention, and degree attainment (Astin, Tsui, & Avalos, 1996). Notably, the vast numbers of minority-serving institutions are privately governed. In terms of community colleges, there remain small enclaves of historically Black and women's two-year institutions of which many are private colleges. These institutions have unique campus climate and distinct missions to serve special populations. Various institutions of higher learning illustrate aspects of the interconnectedness of culture, identity, and schooling in accord with the tailored aims of their college and constituencies (Rhoads, 1999; Rhoads & Valadez, 1996). Not only does racial and ethnic cultural pluralism (i.e., diversity) shape campus climates, but the institutional type and heterogeneity of student gender, age, and status of enrollment level do as well.

Participation of African Americans and Women in Higher Education

The United States is becoming increasingly multiethnic and changing demographics suggest that during the twenty-first century the term minority will no longer be an appropriate designation as racially diverse groups will collectively represent the majority of the U.S. population (U.S. Bureau of the Census, 1996a). As higher education is commonly thought to be the great societal equalizer, there are differential rates of progression to college by race or ethnicity with substantially higher rates of White high school graduates attending college than African Americans (Solomon & Wingard, 1991). High school completion rates and patterns of postsecondary enrollment among African Americans have fallen in part to a host of factors such as college costs, academic preparedness, and proximity that affect access to higher education (Benjamin, 1996).

With regard to higher education participation, over the last 20 years community colleges have traditionally enrolled higher proportions of African American students than four-year colleges and universities (Rendon & Garza, 1996; Rendon & Matthews, 1994; Solomon & Wingard, 1991). Baccalaureate-degree granting institutions' total enrollment in 1997 comprised 10% African American students while community colleges' total enrollment consisted of 11% African American (National Center for Educational Statistics, 1999). At present, the majority of educational opportunities for students of color are at community colleges as they enroll almost half of all African American collegians (Rendon & Hope, 1996; Townsend, 2000).

Considering higher education participation by gender, nearly two-thirds of African American undergraduates are women. While the majority of African Americans are in two-year institutions, 58% of all community college students are women (Horn & Maw, 1995; American Association of Community Colleges, 2000). Roughly two-thirds of community college students are part-time attendees, of which a significant number are women, many who are not traditional college age (i.e., 18-24) students (Jacobs, 1999; National Center for Educational Statistics, 1997; American Association of Community Colleges, 2000). Full-time, baccalaureate degree aspirants attending two-year institutions are twice as likely as part-timers to transfer to a four-year college or university within five years (National Center for Educational Statistics, 1997). Therefore, the racial/ethnic background, gender and enrollment status of community college students relate to the orientation of those attending, campus climate, institutional culture, and student outcomes.

Clearly, issues revolving around race and gender affect campus climate differently across institutional contexts given the unique student compositions of the various colleges and universities. As such, the remainder of this chapter addresses the defining mission and characteristics of two-year institutions. More specifically, the following section gives attention to the multi-faceted nature of American community colleges founded to further postsecondary educational attainment among underrepresented, disenfranchised African Americans and women.

Historical Origins and Unique Missions: Two- and Four-Year Black Colleges.

Education has long been viewed as the gateway to upward mobility and economic independence. Not limited to the area of education, the history of African Americans in the United States is replete with instances of overt discriminatory treatment along color lines. Unlike other racial/ethnic groups, many African Americans did not immigrate to the United States, but were brought to this country against their will and sold into slavery (Bennett, 1988; Bonacich, 1989). Treated as subhuman, traditional practice was to keep African Americans from receiving schooling.

While very few White institutions admitted African Americans in the late nineteenth century, the few that did were located in the North and most African Americans were in the South (Guyden, 1999). Though against the law to educate persons of African decent, abolitionists and missionaries founded schools for African Americans during the late 1800s in an effort to extend postsecondary opportunities to those with collegiate aspirations (Guyden, 1999). Several educational foundations were established for African Americans between the Civil War and World War I (Bowman, 1992). With the second Morrill Act of 1890, public land-grant institutions of higher learning were established for African Americans, which launched legal racial separation of colleges and universities, particularly in the south.

Often referred to as 'Historically Black Colleges and Universities' (HBCUs), the curriculum initially had a vocational emphasis that later evolved to include and promote general/liberal arts studies (Guyden, 1999). By 1900, roughly 100 HBCUs had been established, the majority as four-year institutions (Townsend, 1999). Despite institutional attrition, at present there still exist approximately 107 HBCUs in the United States comprising 9% of baccalaureate-granting institutions, many which are privately controlled (Bowman, 1992; Hope, 1996). Although 75% of African American students attend predominately White institutions (PWIs), HBCUs have consistently produced slightly over one-third of African American bachelor degree recipients, outproducing other institutional types (Chideya, 1995; Hope, 1996). For that reason, there are significant differences in the educational outcomes for African American students at traditional Black colleges and universities versus PWIs (Jackson & Swan, 1991).

Similar to historically Black four-year institutions, Black two-year colleges carried the same charge of providing ex-slaves educational opportunities. Most two- and four-year Black institutions of higher learning were church affiliated colleges and many were extensions of segregated secondary schools (Guyden, 1999; Hope, 1996). In describing characteristics of HBCUs in general, Clayton (1979) reported that 42% of Black colleges are located in cities with fewer than 50,000 people; many that are religious-affiliated are Methodist; and 84% of those accredited are in the southern association. Different from historically Black four-year colleges and universities, the development of Black two-year institutions was an outgrowth of the twentieth century (Townsend, 1999). Lane (1933, in Guyden, 1999), made an early attempt to provide a portrait of historically Black two-year colleges, noting that these institutions largely promoted a liberal arts curriculum with the purpose of encouraging transfer in pursuit of baccalaureate degrees. For that reason, degrees conferred at four-year institutions held more prestige, placing little emphasis on vocational education within Black two-year colleges irrespective of open admissions policies as the general rule for each tier.

As the educational aspirations and academic needs of African American students' further convoluted attempts to equalize post-secondary schooling, various threats to the existence of HBCUs, particularly two-year institutions, arose. While at one time well over 100 Black colleges were two-year institutions or provided two-year curriculums, by the late 1970s severe declines were witnessed (Guyden, 1999; Historically Black colleges and universities fact book, 1983). By 1997, only fourteen historically Black, two-year institutions remained, most located in the Southeast. Attendance at eleven of these institutions range from just short of 200 students to over 1,700[1] (Townsend, 1999).

Unfortunately, due to the higher costs of a private college education, many African American students cannot afford to attend these institutions specifically founded to foster their educational attainment, as nearly two-thirds are privately controlled (Hope, 1996). In contrast to those educated in public HBCUs, African American private college students have degree aspirations that exceed the baccalaureate level, higher grade point averages, and better academic progression (Davis & Nettles, 1987; Horn & Maw, 1995). Although both public and private HBCUs combined account for less than 9% of postsecondary institutions, publicly controlled PWIs, particularly public two-year colleges, may be the first-choice, or only option, for postsecondary attendance among low-income and first generation students in pursuit of the baccalaureate degree.

Predominantly Black institutions (PBIs) have emerged which, unlike HBCUs, were not originally erected with the sole purpose of educating African Americans, but arose from traditional White institutions that, over time, witnessed growth in African American student attendees who comprise at least 50% of total enrollment (Guyden, 1999; Townsend, 1999). While HBCUs are geographically located primarily in the Southern states, in contrast, PBIs are often in major cities. Likewise, two-year PBIs are metropolitan community colleges with 50% or greater African American enrollment; whereas Black-serving institutions have student bodies that enroll between 25% to 49% African Americans (Townsend, 1999). While the majority of students at historically Black and predominantly Black two-year colleges are African American, the same degree of diversity does not exist in terms of faculty at these institutions, as over one-quarter are White (Foster, Guyden, & Miller 1999).

Given the relatively small number of Black community colleges, both historically Black and predominantly White institutions of higher learning (particularly PWIs enrolling one-quarter or more African Americans) should work cooperatively to address high attrition, low rates of transfer, declines in the number of associate degrees awarded to African Americans, and subsequent transition to the baccalaureate (Simmons & Jackson, 1988). Relative to college choice, cost and location are major factors for African Americans considering higher learning. Due to lower tuition rates, institutions that are within an individual's financial reach and in close proximity are commonly community colleges.

Many urban community colleges boast large enrollments and research has noted that the size and level of an institution can adversely impact student aspirations (Carter, 1999). Irrespective of the tier, large student enrollments hinder students' level of comfort within the institutional environment, preventing them from self-actualizing, thereby slowing their academic progression (Attinasi, as cited in Carter, 1999). Critics contend that community colleges are not the optimal environment for those seeking baccalaureate degree completion (Brint & Karabel, 1989; Clark; 1960; Karabel, 1986; Dougherty, 1987, 1994; Pascarella et al.,

1998; Pincus & Archer, 1989; Whitaker & Pascarella, 1994). Nonetheless, African American and female students are commonly left little choice in utilizing two-year institutions as the conduit to a bachelor's degree.

Providing Educational Access for American Indians: The Tribal College

In a relatively short period of time, tribal colleges have improved the educational opportunities of American Indian students who otherwise might not have participated in higher education. These schools are unique institutions that blend the traditional community college goals of local economic development, workforce training, and preparation for continuing education with a combination of supplemental student support, cultural preservation and enhancement, and community outreach. As Boyer (1997) notes in his report on American Indian Colleges, "tribal colleges establish a learning environment that supports students who had come to view failure as the norm"(p. 4). These schools have succeeded despite a host of obstacles that include a chronic lack of funding, dilapidated facilities, and the low-income levels and poor academic preparation of many of their students (Boyer, 1997).

Probably the most important function of the tribal college is the access it provides for students – especially local ones – who otherwise would not participate in higher education (Boyer, 1997). To help students with their family responsibilities, colleges such as Fond du Lac, Little Big Horn, and Fort Peck operate on-site daycare centers for the children of students, and these centers are often available to the wider community as well (American Indian College Fund, 1996). Besides their open admissions policies and convenient locations, some colleges offer transportation to and from isolated parts of the reservation, while others have decentralized their campuses – in effect "moving classes to the students" (Cahape & Howley, 1992, p. 98). For example, Bay Mills Community College has offered classes at each of the twelve reservations in Michigan since 1984; Oglala Lakota has established a college center in each of the nine districts of the Pine Ridge reservation; and Sitting Bull College operates an innovative adult learning program that features a mobile classroom to serve outlying districts (American Indian College Fund, 1996).

Because tribal colleges often serve academically unprepared students who are forced to deal with family responsibilities, financial difficulties, and other problems, providing access is not enough (Cunningham & Parker, 1998). The colleges, therefore, continue supporting their students after enrollment by offering tutoring programs that build basic skills, General Education Development (GED) instruction, as well as active counseling programs for students. Faculties consciously try to develop self-esteem in students as "the greatest obstacle is often psychological – the belief that higher education is something foreign and intimidating" (Boyer, 1997, p. 58). In addition, many tribal colleges work with local four-year institutions to ensure that courses are comparable and that the transfer process goes smoothly for those students who decide to continue their education. For example, the College of the Menominee Nation has articulation agreements with the University of Wisconsin at Stevens Point and Green Bay and Wisconsin's Technical Colleges in Wausau, Appleton, and Green Bay, to facilitate student transfers (American Indian College Fund, 1996).

Tribal colleges also utilize distance learning to encourage access and persistence toward a degree. All tribal colleges participate in a network that allows them to increase the number of courses they can offer by downloading them from other sites via satellite. Several of the colleges – including Lac Courte Oreilles and Blackfeet – offer courses from state institutions through video, audio, and other digital communications, thereby providing students with the opportunity to complete undergraduate degrees without leaving the reservation.

Hispanic-Serving Institutions: High-Serving Institutions

In order to understand the barriers that are involved in educating the U.S. Hispanic population, it is important to realize that Hispanics are, by no means, a homogeneous group. The use of the term *Hispanic* – and, more recently, *Latino* – within the United States are both umbrella terms that represent many national races, cultures, and origins. These individuals represent descendants of pre-Columbian inhabitants of the Americas to the offspring of migratory streams to the Spanish-speaking New World. The United States' Hispanic population also includes sixth- and seventh-generation U.S. citizens.

The continued influx of Hispanics has perpetuated the division between the dominant Anglo culture and the ethnic and socioeconomic stereotypes of Hispanics as newly arrived, non-English-speaking, illegal aliens. According to the President's Advisory Commission on Educational Excellence for Hispanic Americans (1996), approximately 64% of the Hispanic population in the United States is made up of U.S. born citizens. While a growing number of Hispanics have achieved economic success in the United States and interact with ease in English-speaking circles, Hispanics are often portrayed in the media and in public discourse as unassimilated, undereducated, child-laden, and menially employed.

Although Hispanics are the fastest growing minority in the United States, their numbers at all levels of the educational system in this country have not kept pace with their population growth. Dropout rates for Hispanics are higher and occur earlier than for other ethnic groups. The President's Advisory Commission on Educational Excellence for Hispanic Americans (1996) reports that "40% of 16- to 24-year-old Hispanic dropouts left school with less than a 9th grade education, compared with 13% of White dropouts and 11% of Black dropouts" (p. 26). The National Education Goals Panel (1996) points out that in 1995 the disparity between Whites and Hispanics with regard to high school completion was 27%, while it was 5% between Whites and Blacks. Disparities in college completion rates between Whites and Hispanics are also growing. In 1992, the gap between the proportions of Hispanic and White high school graduates who completed a college degree was 15%; in 1996, the gap was 21%.

Within less than a decade, however, Hispanic enrollment in postsecondary institutions nearly doubled from 520,000 in 1992 to 1,045,600 in 1997. Hispanic students account for 9% of the nation's fifteen million students in postsecondary institutions (O'Brien & Zudak, 1998), up from 4.5% in 1985. According to the U.S. Department of Education's Fact Sheet on Title III Institutions (1998), more than half of Hispanics in postsecondary education are concentrated in about 177 institutions with 25% or more Hispanic enrollment.

An Overview of HSIs. The term *Hispanic-serving institution* (HSI) is a relatively recent educational classification that has yet to be uniformly defined. "The most frequently used criterion to identify HSIs is a Hispanic student enrollment of 25% or more" (Benitez, 1998, p. 59). Title III of the Higher Education Act (HEA) of 1965 provides the most important, as well as the most restrictive, legal definition of a HSI (U.S. Department of Education, 1997). Title III authorized federal aid programs to institutions that served large numbers of needy and underrepresented students. According to Title III, Section 312 of the HEA, to be eligible for aid, institutions must meet the following criteria:

- Cannot be for-profit;
- Must offer at least two-year academic programs that lead to a degree;
- Must be accredited by an accrediting agency or association recognized by the Secretary of Education;
- Must have a high enrollment of economically needy students; and
- Must have low-average education expenditures.

In addition to meeting these criteria, to be recognized as an HSI an institution must:

- Have at least 25% Hispanic undergraduate full-time-equivalent (FTE) student enrollment;
- Provide assurances that no less than 50% of its Hispanic students are low-income individuals and first-generation college students; and
- Provide assurances that an additional 25% of its Hispanic students are low-income individuals or first-generation college students.

Other entities including the White House Initiative on Educational Excellence for Hispanic Americans and the Hispanic Association of Colleges and Universities employ criteria that are similar to, but less exacting than, Title III to identify HSIs. They define HSIs as accredited degree-granting public or private non-profit institutions of higher education with at least 25% Hispanic student enrollment. This definition increases the number of HSIs from 131 to 177, based on Integrated Postsecondary Education Data System (IPEDS) for 1995-96. This definition, however, does not have legal status. Federal agencies and other funding sources tend to rely on existing statutes when developing policy directives and funding priorities. "At present, the only statutory references to HSIs is the HEA Title III definition" (Benitez, 1998, p. 60).

The development of most HSIs has taken place within the last three decades. This development is closely related to two extraordinary quantitative increases that have brought about qualitative changes in education in the United States – a large increase in federal funding, and a dramatic increase in the Hispanic population of the United States. The great increase in need-based federal student aid that followed the passage in 1965 of the Higher Education Act (HEA) allowed more student access to postsecondary education. Far more important than Title III to the development of HSIs and other minority serving institutions were the programs that were created under Title IV of the HEA. Title IV established the Basic Educational Opportunity Grants, which later became Pell grants, as well as college work-study and guaranteed student loan programs. Federal student grants, along with the movement for open admissions, were the keys to the gates of higher education for U.S. minority populations.

Today's Profile of the HSI. The most frequent type of institution among HSIs is a public two-year community college that is greatly dependent on state and federal funds, and that has a limited budget with almost no endowment. According to the U.S. Department of Education (1997):

- The total revenues of HSIs are 42%, or $5,742, less per FTE student than at other institutions;
- Endowment revenues at HSIs per FTE student are 91% less than at other institutions;
- HSIs spend 43% less on instruction per FTE student than other schools;
- HSIs spend 51% less on academic support functions (i.e., libraries, curriculum development, etc.) per FTE student than other schools; and
- HSIs spend 27% less on student services (guidance, counseling, financial aid administration, etc.) per FTE student than other schools.

The financial condition of a large number of HSIs is precarious. Many HSIs are underequipped, understaffed, unable to competitively hire, develop baccalaureate or graduate programs, maintain modern research facilities, or offer high-tech learning and working environments. Given this current picture, one wonders whether Hispanic students are better off at HSIs than at other institutions that are stronger financially and academically. However, it is important to consider the profile of today's typical Hispanic student.

Hispanic students tend to be enrolled part-time in an associate or nondegree program near their home. They often receive federal student aid mainly in the form of Pell grants and must work in order to stay in school. Hispanic students usually take longer than Whites to complete a degree and are 33% more likely than Whites to drop out before completing a bachelor's degree (U.S. Department of Education, 1997). Financial factors, including tuition costs, availability of financial aid, and nearness to home are major considerations for Hispanic students when choosing a school.

HSIs are both relatively inexpensive and close to home for most Hispanic students. Despite their limitations, the rate of completion for Hispanic students at HSIs is higher than at majority institutions. According to the U.S. Department of Education (1997) "whereas 32% of all Hispanic students in higher education are enrolled at [Title III] HSIs, Hispanic students at HSIs earn 47% of the associate degrees and 48% of the bachelor's degrees awarded to Hispanic students nationwide" (p. 2). HSIs figure prominently as part of the top one hundred schools that grant the highest number of bachelor degrees to Hispanics. However, they lose ground at the masters' level and practically disappear from the doctoral listing. As noted earlier, most HSIs offer only undergraduate degrees and most are two-year institutions.

HSIs have begun to use statistics to request increased government funding as well as to gain credibility as a successful educational alternative for minorities. Not exclusively Hispanic, a large number of HSIs also serve other minority populations, with more than 65% of the students enrolled at HSIs belonging to diverse minority groups (U.S. Department of Education, 1998).

Not all HSIs were originally founded as Hispanic-serving institutions. Migratory and demographic shifts have helped to redefine the student population at many campuses throughout the United States. This means that HSIs were not necessarily designed or staffed with a Hispanic student population in mind. It may be argued that the fact that an institution enrolls large numbers of Hispanic students need not imply or assure that it is geared to their educational needs. A closer examination of individual institutions is required to ascertain their effectiveness, taking into account their mission, student populations, academic offerings and achievements, faculty and staff profiles, student support services, funding sources, and funding priorities.

Nevertheless, it is still fair to say that HSIs as a group are presently at the front line of American postsecondary education. They are dealing with the population mix that will dominate the twenty-first century, and appear to be doing better than any groups' institutions at meeting the educational needs of Hispanics. Whether their efforts and resources suffice to meet the challenge of educating Hispanics in the United States is another question. HSIs, at present, are seriously underfunded, and most do not go beyond the undergraduate level. That is not sufficient to serve the needs of the population, or of the nation in the future.

Many HSIs are part of community college systems and are assigned their mandates and funds by a central administrative office, which, in turn, answers to city authorities or state legislatures. Thus, the level of funding most HSIs receive is tied to the political process at the local, state, and federal levels and ebb and flow of the clout and networking skills of the representatives of Hispanic communities.

Evolution and Challenges in Continuance of Two-year Women's Colleges

Prior to the nineteenth century, women were educationally disadvantaged as societal roles dictated that only White men should receive formal postsecondary education. Participation of women of Anglo decent in higher education was witnessed as early as 1749 via women's seminaries (Kelly, 1987; Schuman & Olufs, 1995). However, it was not until the early 1800s that the educational training of White women gained social acceptance. More significant, by 1920 women made up 47% of college undergraduates (Lerner, 1993).

During the 1930s there were 211 two- and four-year women's colleges, accounting for 16% of all higher education institutions. It is estimated that as many as 80 two-year women's colleges existed in 1940, the majority religiously affiliated and privately controlled (Wolf-Wendel & Pedigo, 1999). Moreover, between

1930 and 1976, 40% of women's colleges were two-year institutions (Wolf-Wendel & Pedigo, 1999).

Wolf-Wendel and Pedigo (1999) reported that there were 252 women's colleges in 1960, but by 1993 roughly two-thirds of institutions for women had disappeared. The institution of choice during the first half of the 1900s in the Northeast and South, women's colleges began to lose momentum with the growth of coeducational institutions, especially public colleges and universities (Townsend, 1999; Wolf-Wendel & Pedigo, 1999). Women's colleges also reached a stalemate in terms of further development and longevity due to many becoming four-year institutions (Schultz & Stickler, 1965).

Two-year colleges specifically for women were thought appropriate as women frequently stayed home while pursuing additional education. However, Solomon (1985) suggested that two-year women's colleges were enacted as a means of stratifying educational opportunity by gender. In other words, men would be able to attend senior level institutions leading to higher degrees while women would have less access to four-year colleges and universities.

Presently, the majority of college students earning two-year and bachelors degrees are female (Jacobs, 1999). Similar to persons of color, women are overrepresented in community colleges in general, concurring with Solomon's assertions regarding the educational stratification of women in higher education (Jacobs,1999; American Association of Community Colleges, 2000). Although the majority of women attend coeducational institutions of higher learning, as of 1997 there were over 80 women's colleges, of which only five were two-year institutions.

In contrast to two-year Black colleges, less has been written about two-year womens' institutions of higher learning. Existing literature on women's colleges is contradictory regarding the effects of single-sex postsecondary education on student outcomes. Some researchers (Miller-Bernal, 1989; Riordan, 1994; Smith, 1990) contend there are significant positive effects while others insist womens' colleges bear no influence on student outcomes (Gose, 1995; Stoecker & Pascarella, 1991). Robinson (1990) suggests that at the core of single-sex education for women are leadership and self-esteem building skills that are generally negated in coeducational college choices. Hence, women's colleges can provide particularly laudable contributions in the personal and professional development of female students. However, given declining enrollments at single-sex institutions and the virtual extinction of two-year women's colleges, the extent to which collegiate education of this kind can be nurtured is daunting (Gose, 1995; Perry, 2000).

Conclusion

Minority-serving institutions (MSI) have clearly helped to fulfill the vast educational needs of a growing number of language and cultural minorities. Their convergent strengths have supported the economic development and social mobility of people of color and women as mainstream institutions historically have provided similar opportunities for the majority population. MSIs collectively share a number of characteristics that have contributed significantly to the educational development of racial and ethnic groups in the United States. Included among these strengths are:

- Their collective, targeted missions;
- The significant number of degrees conferred each year;
- Culturally based educational efforts;
- Various leadership opportunities;
- Independent and self-sufficient daily operations; and
- Educational, economic, and community development endeavors.

The stated missions of these schools address the issues that form a well-recited litany of the failures that characterize many mainstream institutions in their attempts to educate minorities and women. Recognizing that mainstream institutions were built for nonminority populations and women, MSIs have attempted to structure and organize education experiences for students within their own social and cultural contexts.

Notes

1. As reported, enrollment information was not provided for three institutions as they were community colleges with one or more branch campuses.

References

Adelman, C. (1999). *Answers in the toolbox: Academic intensity, attendance patterns, and bachelor's degree attainment.* Washington, DC: U. S. Department of Education.

American Association of Community Colleges. (2000). *National profile of community colleges: Trends and statistics (3rd ed).* Washington, DC: Community College Press.

American Association of Community Colleges. (1998). *Pocket profile of community colleges: Trends and statistics 1997-1998.* Washington, DC: Community College Press.

American Council on Education. (2000). *Minorities in higher education 1999-2000.* Washington, DC: American Council on Education.

American Indian College Fund (AICF). (1996, November). *Unpublished profiles of tribal colleges.*

Aragon, S. R. (Ed.). (2000). *Beyond access: Methods and models for increasing retention and learning among minority students.* San Francisco: Jossey-Bass.

Astin, A. W., Tsui, L. & Avalos, J. (1996). *Degree attainment rates at American colleges and universities: Effects of race, gender, and institutional type.* Los Angeles, CA: Higher Education Research Institute, University of California, Los Angeles.

Benjamin, M. (1996). *Cultural diversity, educational equity, and the transformation of higher education: Group profiles as a guide to policy and programming.* Westport, CT: Greenwood.

Benitez, M. (1998). Hispanic-serving institutions: Challenges and opportunities. In J. P. Merisotis & C. T. O'Brien (eds.). *Minority-serving institutions: Distinct purposes, common goals* (pp. 57-68). San Francisco: Jossey-Bass.

Bennett, L. Jr. (1988). *Before the Mayflower: A history of black America,* (6th ed.) New York: Penguin Books.

Bonacich, E. (1989). Inequality in America: The failure of the American system for people of color. *Sociological Spectrum, 9,* 77-101.

Bowman, J. W. (1992). *America's black colleges: The comprehensive guide to historically & predominantly black 4-year colleges and universities.* Pasadena, CA: Sandcastle Publishing.

Boyer, P. (1997). *Native American colleges: Progress and prospects.* Princeton, NJ: Carnegie Foundation for the

Advancement of Teaching.

Brint, S. & Karabel, J. (1989). American education, merito-cratic ideology, and the legitimization of inequality: The community college and the problem of American exceptionalism. *Higher Education, 18,* 725-735.

Briscoe, D. B., & Ross, J. M. (1989). Racial and ethnic minorities and adult education. In S. B. Merriam and P. M. Cunningham (eds.), *Handbook of Adult and Continuing Education* (pp. 583-598). San Francisco: Jossey-Bass.

Cahape, P., & Howley, C. B. (eds.). (1992). *Indian nationals at risk: Listening to the people.* Summaries of papers commissions by the Indian Nationals at Risk Task Force of the U.S. Department of Education. Charleston, WV: Clearinghouse on Rural Education and Small Schools.

Carter, D. F. (1999). The impact of institutional choice and environments on African-American and White students' degree expectations. *Research in Higher Education, 40,* 17-41.

Chideya, F. (1995). *Don't believe the hype: Fighting cultural misinformation about African Americans.* New York: Penguin.

Cohen, A. M. & Brawer, F. B. (1996). *The American community college* (3rd ed.). San Francisco, CA: Jossey-Bass.

Clark, B. (1960). The "cooling out" function in higher education. *American Journal of Sociology,* 65, 569-576.

Clayton, R. (1979). *Some characteristics of the historically black colleges.* (ED176651)

Cunningham, A. F., & Parker, C. (1998). Tribal colleges as community institutions and resources. In J. P. Merisotis, & C. T. O'Brien (eds.), *Minority-serving institutions: Distinct purposes, common goals* (pp. 45-56). San Francisco: Jossey-Bass.

Davis, J. E. & Nettles, M. T. (1987). *Academic progression of students at public and private historically black colleges.* Paper presented at the Annual Meeting of the Association for the Study of Higher Education, San Diego, CA. (ED281462).

Dougherty, K. (1987). The effects of community colleges: Aid or hindrance to socioeconomic attainment? *Sociology of Education, 60,* 86-103.

Dougherty, K. J. (1994). *The contradictory college: The conflicting origins, impacts, and future of the community college.* New York: State University of New York.

Foster, L., Guyden, J. A., & Miller, A. L. (1999). *Affirmed action: Essays on the academic and social lives of white faculty members at historically black colleges and universities.* New York: Rowman & Littlefield.

Gose, B. (1995, Februrary). Second thoughts at women's colleges. *Chronicle of Higher Education, 41*(22), A22-24.

Guyden, J. A. (1999). Two-year historically black colleges. In B. K. Townsend (Ed.), *Two-year colleges for women and minorities: Enabling access to the baccalaureate* (pp. 85-112). New York: Falmer Press.

Historically black colleges and universities fact book, Volume 1: Junior & Community Colleges (1983). Washington, DC: Federal Government, Division of Black American Affairs.

Hoffman, C. M. & Associates (1996). *Historically black colleges and universities, 1976-1994.* Washington, DC: U.S. Government Printing Office. (ED399897)

Hope, R. O. (1996). Revitalizing minority colleges and universities. In . L. I. Rendon & R. O. Hope (eds.), *Educating a new majority: Transforming America's educational system for diversity,* (pp. 390-402). San Francisco, CA: Jossey-Bass.

Horn, L. & Maw, C. (1995). *Minority undergraduate participation in postsecondary education: A statistical report.* Toronto, Ontario: Council of Ontario Universities. (ERIC Document Reproduction Service No. ED383267).

Jacobs, J. A. (1999). Gender and the stratification of colleges. *The Journal of Higher Education, 70* (2), 161-187.

Jackson, K. W. & Swan, L. A. (1991). Institutional and individual factors affecting black undergraduate student performance: Campus race and student gender. In W. R. Allen, E. G. Epps, & N. Z. Haniff (eds.), *College in black and white: African American students in predominantly white and in historically black public universities* (pp. 127-141). New York: SUNY.

Karabel, J. (1986). Community colleges and social stratification in the 1980s. *New Directions for Community Colleges, 54,* 13-30.

Katsinas, S. G. (1993, April). *Toward a classification system for community colleges.* Paper presented at Annual Meeting of the Council of Universities and Colleges Portland, OR.

Kelly, D. K. (1987). *The nineteenth century experience of women college students: A profile of the women and their motivations.* (ED292745)

Lerner, G. (1993). *The creation of feminist consciousness:*

From the middle ages to eighteen-seventy. New York: Oxford University Press.

Merisotis, J. P. & O'Brien, C. T. (eds.). (1998). *Minority-serving institutions: Distinct purposes, common goals*. San Francisco: Jossey-Bass.

Miller-Bernal, L. (1989). College experiences and sex-role attitudes: Does a women's college make a difference? *Youth and Society, 20*(4), 363-387.

National Center for Educational Statistics (1997). *Transfer behavior among beginning postsecondary students: 1989-94*. Washington, DC: U.S. Department of Education, Office of Educational Research and Improvement.

National Center for Educational Statistics (1999). *Integrated postsecondary education data system (IPEDS) fall enrollment survey*. Washington, DC: U. S. Department of Education.

National Education Goals Panel. (1996). *The national education goals report: Building a nation of learners*. Washington, DC: Government Printing Office.

O'Brien, E. M., & Zudak, C. (1998). Minority-serving institutions: An overview. In J. P. Merisotis & C. T. O'Brien (eds.), *Minority-serving institutions: Distinct purposes, common goals* (pp. 5-15). San Francisco: Jossey-Bass.

Pascarella, E. T., Edison, M., Nora, A., Hagedorn, L. S., & Terenzini, P. T. (1998). Does community college attendance versus four-year college attendance influence students' educational plans? *Journal of College Student Development, 39*(2), 179-193.

Peeke, G. (1994). *Mission and change: Institutional mission and its application to the management of further and higher education*. Bristol, PA: SRHE & Open University Press.

Perry, P. (2000). *Culture at the crossroads: The education of women: Is there a future for women's colleges in the new millennium?* Paper presented at the Technological Education and National Development (TEND) Conference, Abu Dhabi, United Arab Emirates. (ERIC Document Reproduction Service No. ED447279).

Pincus, F. & Archer, E. (1989). *Bridges to opportunity: Are community colleges meeting the transfer needs of minority students?* New York: Academy for Educational Development and College Entrance Examination Board.

President's Advisory Commission on Educational Excellence for Hispanic Americans. (1996). *Our nation on the fault line:*

Hispanic American education. Washington, DC: Government Printing Office.

Quality Education for Minorities Project (1990). *Education that works.* Cambridge, MA: MIT.

Rendon, L. I. & Matthews, T. B. (1994). Success of community college students: Current Issues. In J. L. Ratcliff, S. Schwarz, & L. H. Ebbers (eds.), *Community Colleges: ASHE Reader Series* (pp. 343-353). Needham Heights, MA: Simon & Schuster Custom Publishing.

Rendon, L. I. & Garza, H. (1996). Closing the gap between two- and four-year institutions. In L. I. Rendon & R. O. Hope (eds.), *Educating a new majority: Transforming America's educational system for diversity* (pp.289-308). San Francisco, CA: Jossey-Bass.

Rendon, L. I., & Hope, R. O. (1996). An educational system in crisis. In L. I. Rendon & R. O. Hope (eds.), *Educating a new majority: Transforming America's educational system for diversity* (pp. 1-32). San Francisco: Jossey-Bass.

Rhoads, R. A. (1999). The politics of culture and identity: Contrasting images of multiculturalism and monoculturalism. In K. M. Shaw, J. R. Valadez, & R. A. Rhoads (eds.), *Community colleges as cultural texts: Qualitative explorations of organizational student culture* (pp. 103-124). New York: State University of New York Press, Albany.

Rhoads, R. A & Valadez, J. R. (1996). *Democracy, multi-culturalism, and the community college: A critical perspective.* New York: Garland.

Richardson, R. C. & Bender, L. W. (1987). *Fostering minority access and achievement in higher education: The role of urban community colleges and universities.* San Francisco, CA: Jossey-Bass.

Richardson, R. C. & Skinner, E. F. (1992). Helping first-generation minority students achieve degrees. *New Directions for Community Colleges, 80,* 29-43.

Riordan, C. (1994). The value of attending a women's college: Education, occupation, and income benefits. *Journal of Higher Education, 65*(4), 486-510.

Robinson, P. W. (1990). *A study of declining enrollment trends in women's colleges in America, and the impact of Brenau College: Emergence of higher education in America.* (ED323863)

Schultz, R. E. & Stickler, W. H. (1965). Vertical extension

of academic programs in institutions of higher education. *Educational Record*, 231-241.

Schuman, D. & Olufs, D. (1995). *Diversity on campus.* Boston, MA: Allyn & Bacon.

Simmons, B. R. & Jackson, A. (1988, March). *Fostering black student enrollment at community colleges and historically black colleges in the same service area.* Paper presented at the National Association for Equal Opportunity in Higher Education, Conference, Washington, DC. (ED301240)

Smith, D. (1990). Women's colleges and coed colleges: Is there a difference for women? *Journal of Higher Education, 61*(2), 181-97.

Solomon, B. M. (9185). *In the company of educated women: A history of women and higher education in America.* New Haven, CT: Yale University Press.

Solomon, L. C. & Wingard, T. L. (1991). The changing demographics: Problems and opportunities. In P. G. Altbach and K. Lomotey (eds.), *The racial crisis in American higher education* (pp. 19-42). Albany, NY: SUNY Press.

Stoecker, J. L. & Pascarella, E. T. (1991). Women's colleges and women's career attainments revisited. *Journal of Higher Education, 62*(4), 394-406.

Townsend, B. K. (1999). Collective and distinctive patterns of two-year special focus colleges. In B. K. Townsend (ed.), *Two-year colleges for women and minorities: Enabling access to the baccalaureate* (pp. 3-42). New York: Falmer Press.

Townsend, B. K. (2000). Integrating nonminority instructors into the minority environment. In S. R. Aragon (Ed.), *Beyond access: Methods and models for increasing retention and learning among minority students* (pp. 85-93). San Francisco: Jossey-Bass.

U. S. Bureau of Census. (1996a). *Current population reports* (pp. 1). Washington, DC: U.S. Department of Commerce.

U. S. Bureau of Census. (1996b). *Population projections of the United States by age, sex, race, and Hispanic origin: 1995 to 2050.* Washington, DC: U. S. Department of Commerce.

U. S. Bureau of Census. (1998). *Age, sex, race, and Hispanic origin reports* (pp. 2-3). Washington, DC: U.S. Department of Commerce.

U. S. Department of Education. (1998). *Fact sheet: Title III institutions.* Washington, DC: Government Printing Office.

U. S. Department of Education. (1997). *Hispanic-serving institutions: An analysis of higher education institutions eligible for the Hispanic-serving institutions program, title III of the higher education act of 1965, as amended.* Unpublished paper.

Whitaker, D. G. & Pascarella, E. T. (1994). Two-year college attendance and socioeconomic attainment. *Journal of Higher Education, 65*(2), 194-210.

Wolf-Wendel, L. & Pedigo, S. (1999). Two-year women's colleges: Silenced, fading, and almost forgotten. In B. K. Townsend (Ed.), *Two-year colleges for women and minorities: Enabling access to the baccalaureate* (pp. 43-83). New York: Falmer Press.

CHAPTER 3

OLD IDEOLOGIES, NEW PRACTICES: MISCONCEPTIONS OF ACCESS AND EQUITY OF COMPUTER-BASED DISTANCE EDUCATION

Jeanita W. Richardson

*New digital technologies signal the beginning of a
new, more dynamic and interactive work, with many
different risks and new challenges, just as
Guttenberg's invention of the printing press...*
Hanna, 2000c, p. 16

Distance education is not a new phenomenon. Rather, it is a very old means of delivering instruction to individuals unable or unwilling to attend traditional educational settings. Just as the Guttenberg press created new opportunities and risks by making printed material accessible to learners, the advent of the personal computer and the Internet have again revolutionized the learning exchange. Thanks to new information technologies, vast quantities of data are now available in an instant to place-bound students. However, computer-based distance learning has, in conjunction with its many opportunities, idiosyncratic challenges. While the impact of this technology may be ground-breaking and pose unique challenges to educational institutions, the dilemmas of access and equity for many Americans remain unchanged.

This chapter examines the new practice of offering distance learning via computer technology, which by virtue of the medium, masks recurrent patterns of exclusionary practices in American

49

higher education. In this most recent example of history repeating itself, African-American, Latino, Native American and low-income communities face all too familiar access questions with regard to distance education. Alexander Randall pondered, "What good is freedom of the press if you have no press" (Kahn & Friedman, 1998, p. 168); likewise, what good is computer-based distance education without access to computers and/or the Internet?

Postsecondary institutions offer distance education in many forms to include print, videos, and television programs. However, the recent proliferation of Internet-based courses offered by colleges and universities, the role of technology in the workplace, and the emergence of the "digital divide" give computer-based education delivery particular currency in higher educational settings.

While contemporary interest in distance education is multifaceted, this chapter argues that this latest instructional intervention is rooted in historical patterns of social and cultural reproduction, which are the doorkeepers of access and equity in higher education. As such, theories advanced by Bordieu (1977), Bell (1977), Kahn and Friedman (1998) and Gordon (1999) will help frame computer technology and the Internet as cultural goods used as instruments of social and cultural reproduction. Application of these theories frame the computer as a cultural good, *not* a neutral social instrument blind to gender, race, class, and ethnicity. In this context, computers and the Internet are symbols that yield benefits of both social and cultural capital, which in turn result in opportunity (Bromley, 1998).

One example of the social and cultural consequences of the digital divide is revealed in patterns of computer use and ownership in the United States. Reports present more than sufficient evidence of the widening gap between the technological "haves" and "have-nots." Applied to online distance education, computer-driven instruction, by virtue of the digital divide, will widen rather than narrow the gap that already exists between the economically established and those who possess little or no social, economic, or political capital, namely, communities of color and the poor.

Definitions

Given the common use of the idioms "access," "equity," "the digital divide," "distance education," and "social and cultural capital," definitions are provided for clarity. Access and equity are significant in discussions of distance education in that they speak to the opportunity, or lack of opportunity, experienced by persons of varied ethnicities, gender, and socio-economic backgrounds. More specifically, access, in the case of distance education, is partially determined by the ease of entree to the technology and the skill set necessary to complete courses, commonly referred to as computer literacy. Since online courses and programs in this chapter are supported by traditional colleges and universities, access also refers to the probability that an applicant will possess the historically valued proficiencies and credentials of the admissions process.

Equity speaks to fair practices that rest upon distributive equality. For example, equity supports the allocation of greater resources to areas of greatest need. This concept is quite different from equality, which would define fair treatment as providing the same resources and opportunities to all parties (Gordon & Bonilla-Bowman, 1999). While often used interchangeably, these concepts propose quite different approaches relative to distance education opportunities. For example, computers and Internet access are readily available in many schools that serve middle- and upper-income students. Schools that serve low-income populations, however, tend not to have the infrastructure or hardware that make computer and Internet integration into curricula practical (Norfles, 2001). If two schools, one serving wealthy children and the other serving poor children were given the same amount to invest in technology, the criteria of equality would be met, but, the criteria of equity might not.

Research relative to the digital divide has begun to quantify the need to focus on technological equity as opposed to equality. The digital divide refers to "disparities in the use of personal computers and the Internet [that] fall closely along categories of income, education, age, and race..." (Associated Press, 2000 p. 32). National Public Radio and Harvard's Kennedy School of Government concurred that the digital divide in the United States is primarily a function of income and race (Kappelman, 2000). For example, Whites are two times more likely than minorities to own a computer, even at comparable income levels (Hotz, 1998; Peterson, 2000). Inequities are even more significant when one considers the multiplied disadvantage of poor communities of color. Unfortunately, despite highly publicized digital disparities, the divide is expected to widen rather than narrow in the coming years (United States Internet Council & ITTA Inc., 2000). Whether a function of race, class, or geographic region, mounting evidence confirms the existence of unequal access to and ownership of computers, which mirror historically familiar American trends.

Definitions of distance education and terms used to refer to this instructional intervention vary. Distance education, distance learning, distributed learning are all terms referring to the physical separation of students and teachers for the delivery of instruction (Dede, 2000). For purposes of this chapter, distance education will be defined as

> A system and a process that connects learners with distributed learning resources... [and] is characterized by separation of place and/or time between instruction and learner, among learners, and/or between the learner and learning resources...conducted through one or more media; use of electronic media is not necessarily required. (American Council on Education, 1996, p. 10)

Instruction may be delivered in multiple ways, e.g., radio, videoconferencing, correspondence texts, television or computer. Inherent in each mode are challenges that promote retention or thwart students' proclivity to complete courses. Given the currency of information technologies, such as the computer and the Internet, it is important to consider some of the idiosyncratic and familiar aspects of access and equity of computer-based distance education.

Finally, social and cultural reproduction in the context of this chapter, aligns with Bourdieu's (1977) notion that power and prestige are passed between empowered agents in society who already, by virtue of group membership, possess some degree of privilege. Social and cultural capital can be considered skills or traits that result from, and perpetuate access to, systems which confer power and preferential treatment.

Cultural and Social Reproduction in Distance Educational Practices

The race for technological proficiency for the poor is similar to, "a hundred yard dash in which one of the runners has his legs shackled together" (Bell, 1977 p. 618). This powerful image captures the essence of access and equity in online distance education. With a personal computer, Internet access, and an understanding of how to use them, the runner, or in this case the learner, proceeds relatively unencumbered. On the other hand, an absence of hardware, computer, and Internet literacy makes the race unfair from the starting block given the shackles of ignorance and the absence of opportunity. Evaluation of these allegorical shackles begins to explicate how social and cultural capital and reproduction negatively impact dispossessed populations in the context of computer-based distance education.

Bourdieu (1977) proposed schools as perpetrators of inequality between social classes. Educational attainment represented the accumulated effects of institutionalized transmission of dominant culture's priorities. As such, even the language of the educational systems, the pedagogical practices, and the tools of communication are grounded in dominant cultural norms, that disproportionately benefit those from the dominanat group. Individuals without access and/or familiarity with these norms are in turn disproportionately disadvantaged.

Kappelman (2000) extends Bourdieu's premise into a critique of the digital divide. He proposed that it is too simplistic to explain the divide with references to equipment and knowing how to negotiate the Web. Instead, technological access and proficiency are the preferred method of information transmission of the dominant culture, which, by design, cripples those without access. Individuals and groups not privy to the volumes of educational and economic opportunities available on the Internet experience the ramifications of the digital divide. In this context, online technology is a cultural good (a valued resource) to be manipulated and controlled. As such, it is consistent with the constructs of social and cultural reproduction.

Since culture is socially constructed by and for members of a dominant group (Gordon, 1999), and since access and proficiency on personal computers have great currency, the marriage of education and technology yields power. Knowledge of and access to modern technology become inextricably linked to social power, and "struggles to expand, change, and control knowledge – and access to it – are struggles to change the control and distribution of power and ultimately the distribution of resources" (Gordon & Bhattacharyya, 1999 p. 168).

Kahn and Friedman (1998) define power as an outgrowth of social interactions which exert themselves coercively or forcibly on others, or noncoercively where individuals or groups in control lead, strongly influence, or control others. Since the assumptions of the dominant culture define and control access not only to technology but also to institutions of higher learning, it is reasonable to assume that the very design of computer-dependent courses offered by conventional postsecondary institutions would manifest itself in an exacerbation of disadvantage.

Power as a benefit of group membership is also related to social and cultural capital. Cultural capital refers to the morals, skills, and practices valued by the dominant group. In other words, group membership affords certain natural exposure that can, and most often does, translates into advantage within a particular society. Social capital is the composite profile individuals bring to the market that would include, for example, education, economic resources, familiarity with marketplace norms and expectations (Bourdieu, 1977).

Possession of cultural and social capital perpetuates access to opportunities to gain more cultural and social capital, creating a cyclical relationship. This cycle of having more, yielding more is the process of reproduction. Social hierarchies are, as a result of reproduction, created with substantively different experience, limits, and exposure between groups with or without access to similar resources (Bourdieu, 1977). Fundamentally then, the evaluation of the cultural and social reproduction influences on education speak to the power relationships between those who already have access to institutions of higher learning and those who have already attained some level of technological proficiency.

Bourdieu (1977) went further and proposed that some consumer goods take on symbolic meaning and are elevated to the status of cultural goods. A cultural good is an object the dominant culture deems worthy of purchase. Those who command sufficient economic resources to secure this symbol of power and access reap social and cultural benefits. Concurring with the view that computers could be cultural goods, Bromley (1998) noted,

> computers, like other technologies, are involved in many ways in the construction and use of power in the way they are designed and built, in how they are sold and to whom and in how they are used...[Thus] the relevant issues are demonstrably not technical ones [but]... social practice. (p.2)

Educational institutions, as described by Bourdieu (1977), are vehicles of dominant culture transmission which perpetuate the divide between the "haves" and "have-nots" in many ways. For example, utilization of Eurocentric pedagogical strategies and online information transmission places certain populations at an intense disadvantage before the educational exchange ever begins. Without access to a computer or the Internet, how would persons know what types of educational opportunities are available? Thus, the system charged with the transmission of knowledge (which in and of itself is popularly viewed as necessary for upward social mobility) uses the language and tools available and familiar to the dominant culture. Despite application of dominant cultural norms and techniques, educational institutions continue to profess a commitment to equal and equitable practices. Equal access and equity, particularly in this context, become fundamentally different conversations. Equality refers to rights to avail oneself of educational opportunities, whereas, equity would focus not only on the opportunity but also on issues of fairness in the selection process.

Pivotal to equity is what Gordon and Bonilla-Bowman (1999) refer to as "distributional appropriateness." An example of distributional appropriateness would be resource allocation based on greatest need, which conflicts with notions of equal opportunity. Stated another way, the argument that there is equal opportunity to secure an adequate education, "denies the precedence of birth, of nepotism, patronage or any other criterion which allocates place..."(Bell, 1977, p. 616) such as class, race, or ethnic group membership. Once again, access and equity to online distance education reflects an ongoing reward of privilege, or social reproduction.

Privilege related to race and opportunity was the focus of a report recently released by the American Educational Research Association.   Race was designated one of the most poignant opportunity markers in American society. Further, contributor William Trent, (as cited in AERA Panel on Racial Dynamics in Colleges and Universities, 2000) indicated,

> Whites as a group have historically been afforded many privileges, ranging from explicit affirmative action to informal networks, through which many opportunities are gained. These often unacknowledged privileges...have resulted in great disadvantages to many minority groups...group membership characteristics, particularly race, continue to determine an individual's experiences and access to opportunities in many ways that have important consequences for academic performance. (pp. 3,4)

Advantages of group membership and class similarly apply as directly to modern technology as higher educational practices as per the U.S. Department of Commerce, National Telecommunications and Information Administration. In a 1999 report entitled, *Falling Through the Net: Defining the Digital Divide*, the following conclusions were presented:

- Urban households with incomes of $75,000 and higher are more than *twenty times* more likely to have access to the Internet than rural households at the lowest income levels, and more than *nine times* as likely to have a computer at home;
- Whites are more likely to have access to the Internet from home than Blacks or Hispanics have from any location;
- Black and Hispanic households are approximately *one-third* as likely to have home Internet access as households of Asian/Pacific Islander descent, and roughly *two-fifths* as likely as White households; [and]
- Regardless of income level, Americans living in rural areas are lagging behind in Internet access. Indeed, at the lowest income levels, those in urban areas are more than twice as likely to have Internet access than those earning the same income in rural areas. (U.S. Department of Com-

merce, National Telecommunications and Information Administration, 1999, p. 1)

These findings concur with numerous findings of reporters and researchers alike that online penetration in the last few years have been confined primarily to the middle- and upper-middle classes (Crockett, 2000; Lach, 2000; Wax, 2000).

Lest there be any question that recent investments in education have narrowed the gap between the technological "haves" and "have-nots," the U.S. Department of Commerce, National Telecommunications and Information Administration. (1999) report went on to convey:

- The gaps between White and Hispanic households and between White and Black households, are now approximately five percentage points larger than they were in 1997; [and]
- The digital divides based on education and income level have also increased in the last year alone. Between 1997 and 1998, the divide between those at the highest and lowest education levels increased 25%, and the divide between those at the highest and lowest income levels grew 29%. (p. 1)

The digital divide and its attendant relationship to race, ethnicity, geographic location, and income was predictably framed within the context of cultural and social reproduction. Stark ownership and access statistics are mere consequences of the reproduction cycle. Taken a step further, the cultural goods (personal computers and Internet availability) grant a degree of status, which magnifies disadvantage particularly in distance education. If certain communities of color and the poor are not participating in the distance education boom at the same rates as other groups, the next logical question is, who is participating and what are the barriers to participation?

Online Distance Education and Higher Education

Computer-based distance education perpetuates the historical debate between advocates and opponents of this mode of learning. Some proponents of distance education would argue that online teaching offers quality learning experiences, which do not seek to replace traditional education. Rather, distance opportunities enrich the options available to students whose needs are currently not being met (Keegan, 1996). Others question the quality of distance instruction and the value of degrees earned via computers. Institutional positions relative to distance opportunities, however, should be considered in light of increasing pressure to meet the diverse needs of unprecedented numbers of students seeking post-secondary courses. Several sources of said pressure include competition for students, the changing needs of students rooted in employment, and advancement criteria.

Strained higher educational budgets and changing student and employer demands have encouraged many postsecondary institutions to at least investigate alternative methods of delivering instruction. Consequently, on-line distance education has become a viable strategy to attract students and generate income.

While online courses in the short term are not typically less expensive than traditional instruction, there are indications that cost savings accrue to institutions over time (U.S. Department of Education National Center for Education Statistics, 1999). While not producing windfall profits, a tendency toward money losses for universities also does not seem common. Profit margins seem to be closely coupled to participation rates. For example, a class of fifteen may yield a net loss whereas a class of twenty might yield a significant profit (Carr, 2001). Despite the high start-up costs associated with a computer-based distance course, which can require as much a $2.5 million dollar investment for an entire program (Blumenstyk, 1999), most institutions charge the same tuition to distance and on-site students (U.S. Department of Education, National Center for Education Statistics, 1999).

The rhetorical value of higher education can be found in its functional relationship to economic and employment opportunity. In a technologically driven age, education has become even more significant because of globalized competition. Tertiary institutions, in an increased effort to meet the growing demands of the business community, governmental agencies and students in an era of reduced public funding, must consider innovative instructional strategies, of which computer-based distance education is one (U.S. Department of Education, National Center for Education Statistics. 1997; Hanna, 2000b).

Evidence of distance instruction prevalence can be found in the rate at which institutions are adopting courses and programs. In 1995, 30% of two and four-year postsecondary institutions offered distance courses. Between 1997 and 1998, one third of higher educational institutions, who previously had not engaged in distance education, began offering distance options (Baldi, 2000). By 1998, the number of distance education programs increased by 72% and public institutions surpassed private institutions in distance offerings (Hill, 2000; U.S. Department of Education National Center for Education Statistics, 1999).

Implementation of computer-based distance initiatives have not resulted in a corresponding decrease in demand for traditional instruction (U.S. Department of Education, National Center for Education Statistics, 1999). Interestingly, elite institutions have sparingly engaged in online courses and programs. Colleges and universities in the Northeast, the seat of the Ivy League, were least likely than institutions in other parts of the United States to offer distance options to students (U.S. Department of Education, National Center for Education Statistics, 1999). As evidence of this sentiment, James J. O'Donnell, vice provost and classics professor at the University of Pennsylvania indicated, "We already turn away four out of five people who'd like to take those courses on our campus...so we don't want to dilute their [the courses' and the students'] value" (Allen, 1997 p. 6). Provost O'Donnell's comments reflect the reticence of some colleges and universities to engage in distance education. Ivy League institutions will most likely continue to offer only a few distance courses and programs in an effort to protect the exclusive status of their degrees and the social capital afforded students. However, given the large numbers of students seeking postsecondary degrees, some institutions, such as the University of Maryland, have chosen to actively engage in remote learning programs and courses which consequently put them in competition with an different kind of educational service provider, distance institutions (Carr, 2001).

Distance institutions and traditional postsecondary institutions that offer alternative instructional settings are different in their focus and operations. Distance institutions exclusively or primarily offer degrees and coursework to students in remote locations. Generally, these institutions do not have campuses in the conventional sense, but rather, distribution centers and sites for faculty, technical, and support staff. Since many distance institutions have open admissions policies, barriers to entry are largely technical.

Traditional institutions include community colleges, technical/trade institutes, colleges and universities whose primary mode of instructional delivery is campus based. Conventional post-secondary establishments tend to evaluate distance student applicants by the same criteria as on-campus students. As a result, historical practices that diminish access and equity for communities of color and/or the poor compound technical deficiencies that might make computer-based distance education a genuine means of widening the door to educational opportunity.

Table 1 compares some institutional considerations of on-line distance courses and programs offered by traditional colleges and universities.

Since conventional benchmarks are heavily weighted in distance courses offered by traditional higher educational concerns, four consequential considerations of postsecondary admission remain:

- Admitting the optimal number of students expected to excel;
- Assembly of a diverse class, with diversity including for example, athleticism, artistic potential not necessarily race and class;
- Attracting students most apt to make distinctive contributions academically and professionally; and,
- Admitting students who represent long-standing relationships, loyalties and traditions within the institution (Bowen & Bok, 1998).

Fear of diluting degree currency may be less pressing for some higher educational enterprises, but does remain a concern. Thus, one explanation why postsecondary admissions criteria are difficult to change, even in light of new technology, is the social capital generated for graduates of selective schools (Bowen & Bok, 1998). Despite the proliferation of educational opportunities at largely public institutions, the barriers to distance admissions are identical to the long-standing barriers to entry in higher education faced by low-income populations and communities of color.

Table 1. A Higher Educational Institution Comparison.

Institutional Considerations	Traditional Universities	On-line Distance Education and/or On-line Course Offerings
Philosophy	Students come to campus for instruction	Instruction goes to the student with faculty and student-to-student interaction via the Internet
Mission	Defined by the level of instruction (undergraduate only vs. graduate and undergraduate programs) and selectivity of students and faculty	Almost exclusively focused on an adult clientele with employment development as the goal
Students	Admissions governed by varying degrees of selectivity based on the status of the institution (post-high school, 18 - 24 - year - olds)	Adult employment history and life experiences heavily weighted within the context of the traditional admissions process (adults, non-traditionally aged students, 25 - year - olds and older)

Adapted from Hanna, D. E. (2000a). The Distance Education/Technology-Based Universities. In D. E. Hanna & Associates (Ed.), *Higher Education in an Era of Digital Competition: Choices and Challenges.* (pp. 117-138). Madison: Atwood Publishing.

Race, Class, Computer Literacy and College Preparedness

Since traditional admissions criteria apply to many distance education programs, as reflected in Table 1, focus needs to be directed toward lower school preparation for college to gain a deeper appreciation of how access and equity are impacted. Gains in composite SAT scores and high school graduation rates have not translated into significant representational shifts in four-year postsecondary institutions for the racial and ethnic minorities of note in this chapter (Carter & Wilson, 1996). Latinos, Native Americans, African Americans and low-income populations continue to be underrepresented in traditional colleges when compared to their population-based representation in the college-age student pool. For example, in the 1995-1996 school year, only 41% of Latinos, 40% of African Americans and 29% of Native Americans enrolled in a postsecondary institution immediately after graduating from high school, as opposed to 56% of Whites. These percentages reflected lower participation than representation in the total U.S. population would indicate. Undergraduate distribution by race that same year were 70% White, 1% Native American, 10% Latino and 12% African American (Volle & Federico, 1997).

As per the National Center for Education Statistics (1999) between 1990 and 1996 participation in higher education has not markedly changed in the last decade for Native Americans or African Americans (an increase from .7 to .9% and from 9.0 to 10.5% of the total postsecondary student populations respectively). Hispanic youth, on the other hand, have increased as a percent of the higher education population from 5.7 to 8.1% for the same period.

Admission criteria, such as test scores and advance placement classes continue to narrow opportunity for the fastest growing subdivisions of the population, Latino and African American youth. Part of the disparity between high school graduation rates, SAT scores, and postsecondary attendance lies in the quality of K-12 education. The application process operates on the premise that all students have an opportunity to take advance placement courses, engage in test preparation, and attend schools staffed with appropriately credentialed faculty, which in reality is not always the case.

While being Latino, African American, or Native American does not necessarily mean that students are poor and attend poor schools; there is a concentration of students of color in lowest income quartile (The College Board National Task Force on Minority High Achievement, 1999). Multiplied disadvantage results when one considers that low income students of color are more apt to attend high poverty schools, be taught math and science by teachers not certified in those disciplines, attend schools in disrepair and have significantly lower exposure to computers and the Internet (Cuomo, 1998; Norfles, 2001; U.S. Department of Education, National Center for Education Statistics, 1997). Professions that nearly 94% of America's schools are connected to the Internet (United States Internet Council & ITTA Inc., 2000) mask the distribution of those computers and the true access students have to them. For example, 74% of the wealthiest schools had Internet connections in classrooms, while only 39% of schools that serve primarily economically deprived students had similar access (Peterson, 2000).

The under-representation of poor populations, Native Americans, Latinos, and African Americans in traditional higher education is well documented. While there is a dearth of data on minority participation in distance education, early records reveal that the primary participants of distance education offered by traditional postsecondary enterprises are White middle-class women (Grill, 1999; Hanna, 2000b; Moore, 1998). Given the technological marginalization (Norfles, 2001; Peterson; 2000) and poor academic exposure of poor minority students (Cuomo, 1998; U.S. Department of Education, National Center for Education Statistics, 1997), it is reasonable to suspect that if colleges retain traditional admissions criteria for computer-based distance education programs representation would, at the very least, mirror traditional patterns of inequity.

Attendance in academe is significant not only because of the economic opportunities generated, but also the social and cultural capital graduation affords students of all races and socioeconomic backgrounds (Bowen & Bok, 1998). Admissions policies, the doorkeepers of attendance, are outgrowths of ideologies, preferences and skills valued by the dominant culture, which when applied decrease postsecondary access for some American youth. Being economically and/or educationally disadvantaged significantly diminishes the probability that a student will possess the skills and experiential set valued in the college admissions process. In the case of distance education, limited proficiencies predictably would diminish the prospects of low-income minority students even further in this technologically based instructional delivery system (Chaney, Muraskin, Cahalan, & Goodwin, 1998).

Distance Learners

While some researchers think it is too soon to develop a profile of potential distance learners, a number of characteristics have emerged in populations that complete the courses or programs they begin on the Internet. Table 2 summarizes some of those traits.

Table 2. Distance Learner Completion Profile.

Demographic Information	Personal Factors Influencing Participation	Learning Style
Average age of learner is between 25 and 45	Highly motivated	Task oreinted and focused
Well-educated; some formal postsecondary education	Low need for peer affiliation	Thrive on assignments with concise and clear directions
Middle class and working full time	High level of confidence	Self-directed learners
White, female, married and place bound	Participation in distance education most often related to employment considerations	Proficient readers
More rural residents than urban; tend to live more than 51 miles from institution with which they are engaged	Tend to take classes voluntarily	Technologically proficient

Grill, 1999; Hanna, 2000d; Moore, 1998; Thompson, 1998; Young, 2000

Overwhelmingly, characteristics of individuals most likely to participate in computer-based distance education are those who already have access to traditional institutions of higher learning, females, middle class, well educated, and between the ages of 25 and 45 (Grill, 1999; Hanna, 2000d; Moore, 1998; Thompson, 1998; Young, 2000). If one considers the composite distance learner profile, there is little doubt that distance education in practice fails to open doors to postsecondary participation for individuals ill-equipped for traditional postsecondary settings. Even the modes of instructional delivery are based on presumptions that the students possess certain skills (e.g., proficient readers, self-directed learners, and technologically proficient) that have been nurtured in their lower school experiences.

Even if one argued that the population of distance learners is heterogeneous, patterns of completion indicate that conspicuously absent from participation are low-income and minority individuals. If this instructional technique addresses the needs of individuals for whom higher educational access already exists, computer-based education will not increase participation in populations where higher education enrollment is already low. As a result, either intentionally or inadvertently, current distance educational delivery may increase access for certain sects of the population, while broadening the gap between the educational haves and have-nots (Grill, 1999).

Conclusions and Recommendations

The opportunity to make a difference is here for those who care about lifelong learning, about equity of access, and about opening the academy to new light, new processes, and new ideas. These are the learning challenges of the next century. (Hanna, 2000c p. 16.)

Education in the United States holds as one of its guiding principles equal educational opportunity, notwithstanding that the populations entitled to equal opportunity have changed over time. Another recurrent theme within the educational exchange has been the transmission of the dominant Eurocentric culture (Gordon & Bonilla-Bowman, 1999). These two important premises continue to prevail within technologically driven distance education. As is the case in traditional contexts, equal opportunity arguably exists, but access and equity do not. Transmission of information via the Internet is only accessible to those with the requisite equipment and skills.

Marginal access and equity in computer-based distance education reveals just one of the contributors to the broadening chasm between the technological upper class and underclass. Distance education practices presented in this chapter do not paint an optimistic picture for low-income populations and minority communities. However, this does not have to become reality if the misconceptions and practices relative to access and equity in distance education are addressed.

The first such misconception is that access and equity in distance education pertain only to communities of color. Results of numerous studies concur unremarkably that computer and Internet access are dependent upon economic resources (U.S. Department of Commerce, National Telecommunications and Information Administration, 1999; Norfles, 2001; Peterson, 2000). However, it is not enough that dollars be allocated for the purchase of hardware and software. Pedagogical strategies employed in K-12 schools must adequately prepare students to avail themselves of online courses.

Pedagogical strategies relative to computer use are not similar across income and race categories. Even with access to modern technology, computers and the Internet function differently in varied educational settings, which provides further evidence of these entities as cultural goods. According to Carolyn Breedlove of the National Education Association (cited in Wax, 2000), "kids in the wealthy districts end up having their computers used for higher-order learning skills...those in areas with low-income students use it for drill and practice, and that exacerbates the digital divide" (p. G8). From this observation, we can deduce that access alone will not solve the technological proficiency gap. Interventions need to ensure that students possess the skill set required to pursue and persist to course or program completion (Chaney et al., 1998).

Institutions viewing online technology solely as a transmission vehicle fail to address pervasive inequities relative to low-income and minority populations' technological access and proficiency, i.e., the digital divide (Chute, Thompson, & Hancock, 1999). On the contrary, "the divide isn't just about having hardware, software, and Internet access, but also about knowing how to use these basic tools of the information age" (Kappelman, 2000, p. 262). Without changes in the fundamental paradigms that currently inform admissions, computer-based courses promise to remain the domain of the educated middle class.

While beyond the purview of this chapter, programmatic sensitivity to culturally-based learning styles and the proficiencies requisite for completion will have to be included in the development of computer-based courses designed to broaden access (Sanchez & Gunawardena, 1998). For example, one of the proposed reasons why online courses appeal to the already employed, is the perceived expectation of employment gains as a direct result of attaining more knowledge. Persistence then is related to job prospects for advancement (Hanna, 2000a; Kember, 1989; Moore, 1998). These are concerns that correlate more to adult populations than youngsters just completing high school. Without pedagogical and paradigmatic shifts, the phenomenon of Internet-based courses will contribute to the list of factors that disproportionately shackle low-income populations and communities of color because their specific needs remain ignored.

Ostensibly, online participation is not indicative of shifts to become more inclusive since the populations most apt to take advantage of computer-based courses already possess the technological prowess and credentials within the parameters of traditional measures of competency. Admissions policies that apply to distance education enrollment still tend to be heavily weighted on test performance, class rank, and rigorous curriculum as predictors of college success. While these factors may be predeterminants of success for some sects of the college-age population, they are not necessarily the only determinants for disadvantaged students (Bowen & Bok, 1998; Chaney et al., 1998).

Institutions of higher learning have an unprecedented opportunity given new technology. Whether valued with the same social capital as traditional degrees, or not, computers offer a venue for life-long learning that could potentially benefit learners both personally and professionally. Untold potential will remain untapped unless there is a concerted effort to deconstruct the social and cultural practices that give more to those that have more. True access and equity in computer-based distance education presents a formidable challenge. The question of whether the academy has the will to unshackle the runner or leave the race for technological proficiency and educational opportunity static and, "a hundred yard dash in which one of the runners has his legs shackled together" (Bell, 1977 p. 618) remains to be seen.

References

AERA Panel on Racial Dynamics in Colleges and Universities. (2000,). *Compelling interest: Examining the evidence on racial dynamics in higher education*, Stanford.

Allen, C. (1997, August 10, 1997). The Virtual University. *Washington Post*, pp. 16-19, 33-35. [On-line]: http://www.search. washingtonpost.com/wp-srv/WPlate/1997-08/10/0051-081097- idx.html.

American Council on Education. (1996). *Guiding principles for distance learning in a learning society* . Washington, DC: ACE Central Services.

Associated Press. (2000, June 24). Low-income minorities yet to ride digital wave. *Houston Chronicle, 32.*

Baldi, G. (2000). *ACE fact sheet on higher education: frequently asked questions about distance dducation*. Division of Government and Public Affairs of the American Council on Education [http://www.acenet.edu, September 11].

Bell, D. (1977). On meritocracy and equality. In J. Karabel & A. H. Halsey (Eds.), *Power and ideology in education* (pp. 607-634). New York: Oxford University Press.

Blumenstyk, G. (1999, July 23). Distance learning at the Open University. *The Chronicle of Higher Education, 45,* A35-38.

Bourdieu, P. (1977). Cultural reproduction and social reproduction. In J. Karabel & A. H. Halsey (Eds.), *Power and ideology in education* (pp. 487-510). New York: Oxford University Press.

Bowen, W. G., & Bok, D. (1998). *The shape of the river: Long-term consequences of considering race in college and university admissions*. Princeton: Princeton University Press.

Bromley, H. (1998). Introduction: Data-driven democracy? Social assessment of educational computing. In H. Bromley & M. Apple (Eds.), *Education/Technology/Power: Educational computing as a social practice* (pp. 1-28). Albany: State University of New York.

Carr, S. (2001). Is anyone making money on distance education? *The Chronicle of Higher Education, XLVII* (23), (February 16), A 41-43.

Carter, D. J., & Wilson, R. (1996). *Minorities in higher education* . Washington, D.C.: American Council on Education.

Chaney, B., Muraskin, L., Cahalan, M., & Goodwin, D. (1998). Helping the progress of disadvantaged students in higher education: The federal student support services program. *Educational Evaluation and Policy Analysis, 20*(3), 197-215.

Chute, A. G., Thompson, M. M., & Hancock, B. W. (1999). *The McGraw-Hill Handbook of Distance Learning*. New York: McGraw-Hill.

College Board the National Task Force on Minority High Achievement. (1999). *Reaching the top*. New York: College Entrance Examination Board.

Crockett, R. O. (2000, May 8). How to bridge America's digital divide. *Business Week* (3680), 56.

Cuomo, A. (1998). *The State of the Cities 1998* . Washington, D.C.: U.S. Department of Housing and Urban Development.

Dede, C. (2000). Advanced technologies and distributed learning in higher education. In D. E. H. & Associates (Ed.), *Higher education in an era of digital competition: Choices and challenges* (pp.71-92). Madison: Atwood Publishing.

Gordon, E. W. (1999). *Education & justice: A view from the back of the bus*. New York: Teachers College Press.

Gordon, E. W., & Bhattacharyya, M. (1999). Human diversity, cultural hegemony, and the integrity of the academic canons. In E. W. Gordon (Ed.), *Education & justice: A view from the back of the bus* (pp. 156-171). New York: Teachers College Press.

Gordon, E. W., & Bonilla-Bowman, C. (1999). Equity and social justice in educational achievement. In E. W. Gordon (Ed.), *Education & justice: A view from the back of the bus* (pp. 71-88). New York: Teachers College Press.

Grill, J. (1999). Access to learning: Rethinking the promise of distance education. *Adult Learning, 10*(4), 32.

Hanna, D. E. (2000a). The distance education/technology-based universities. In D.E. Hanna & Associates (Ed.), *Higher education in an era of digital competition: Choices and challenges* (pp.117-138). Madison: Atwood Publishing.

Hanna, D. E. (2000b). Emerging approaches to learning in collegiate classrooms. In D.E. Hanna & Associates (Ed.), *Higher education in an era of digital competition: Choices and challenges* (pp. 45-70). Madison: Atwood Publishing.

Hanna, D. E. (2000c). Higher education in an era of digital competition: Global consequences. In D.E. Hanna & Associates (Ed.), *Higher education in an era of digital competition: Choices and challenges* (pp. 7-44). Madison: Atwood Publishing.

Hanna, D. E. (2000d). New players on the block: For-profit, corporate, and competency-based learning universities. In D.E. Hanna & Associates (Ed.), *Higher education in an era of digital competition: Choices and challenges* (pp. 139-164). Madison: Atwood Publishing.

Hill, M. (2000, May 1). State's university college plans future as 'Virtual U': Distance education of adults is mission. *The Baltimore Sun*, pp. 1A.

Hotz, R. L. (1998, April 17). Study finds racial divide among Internet users. *The Los Angeles Times*, p. 26.

Kahn Jr., P. H., & Friedman, B. (1998). Control and power in educational computing. In H. Bromley & M. Apple (Eds.), *Education/Technology/Power: Educational computing as a social practice* (pp. 157-174). Albany: State University of New York.

Kappelman, L. A. (2000). Closing the digital divide. *Informationweek* (785), p. 262.

Keegan, D. (1996). *Foundations of Distance Education*. (Third Edition ed.). London: Routedge.

Kember, D. (1989). A longitudinal-process model of drop-out from distance education. *Journal of Higher Education, 60*(3), 278-301.

Lach, J. (2000). Crossing the digital divide. *American Demographics, 22*(6), 9-11.

Moore, M. G. (1998). Introduction. In C. C. Gibson (Ed.), *Distance learners in higher education* (pp. 1-8). Madison: Atwood Publishing.

Norfles, N. (2001). *Closing the divide: Technology use in TRIO Upward Bound projects*. Washington, D.C.: National TRIO Clearinghouse & The Center for the Study of Opportunity in Higher Education.

Peterson, M. M. (2000). Net dreams. *National Journal: The Weekly on Politics and Government*(11), 766-772.

Sanchez, I., & Gunawardena, C. N. (1998). Understanding and supporting the culturally diverse distance learner. In C. C. Gibson (Ed.), *Distance learners in higher education* (pp. 47-64). Madison: Atwood Publishing.

Thompson, M. M. (1998). Distance learners in higher education. In C. C. Gibson (Ed.), *Distance learners in higher education* (pp. 9-24). Madison: Atwood Publishing.

U.S. Department of Commerce, National Telecommunications and Information Administration. (1999). *Falling though the net: defining the digital divide (Executive Summary)* (http://www.ntia.doc.gov/ntiahome/fttn99). Washington, DC.

U.S. Department of Education National Center for Education Statistics. (1997). *The Condition Of Education 1997.* Washington, D.C.: U.S. Government Printing Office.

U.S. Department of Education National Center for Education Statistics. (1999). *The Condition of Education 1999: NCES 1999-022.* Washington, D.C.: U.S. Government Printing Office.

United States Internet Council & ITTA Inc. (2000). *State of the Internet* (http://usic.wslogic.com). Washington, D.C.

Volle, K. & Federico, A. (1997). *Missed opportunities: A new look at disadvantaged college aspirants.* Washington, D.C.: Education Resources Institute & The Institute for Higher Education Policy.

Wax, E. (2000, May 17). Across the E-Divide: public and private efforts are trying to bridge the gap between the haves and have-nots. *The Washington Post,* pp. G8.

Young, J. (2000). Dispatches from distance education, where class is always in session. *The Chronicle of Higher Education, XLVI* (26), A41-42.

CHAPTER 4

STUDENTS WITH LEARNING DISABILITIES: PROVIDING ACCESS AND ACCOMMODATION UNDER THE AMERICANS WITH DISABILITIES ACT

Heraldo V. Richards

The year 2000 marked the tenth anniversary of the Americans with Disabilities Act (ADA). In the ten years that the ADA has been in effect, it has served to buttress the rights of individuals with disabilities, particularly in the area of education. Reinforcing and expanding protections under Section 504 of the Rehabilitation Act of 1973, the ADA has enhanced the rights of students with disabilities. While the ADA has affected every level of education as well as all segments of society, it has made a profound impact on postsecondary education. Addressing rights of access and accommodation, the ADA prescribes equitable treatment of students with disabilities by colleges and universities. Where once physical barriers and institutional practices restricted full participation in college life for students with disabilities, now legislation requires educational institutions to ensure that students with disabilities have access to all programs, activities, and services, and that evaluation of these students be fair, accurate, and nondiscriminatory. Certainly, all students with disabilities are affected by this mandate. However, the largest group of students to benefit from the ADA has been individuals with learning disabilities. Rapidly increasing in their numbers (Gregg & Scott, 2000;Vogel, Leyser, Wyland, & Brulle, 1999), students with learning disabilities, by some estimates, comprise nearly 50% of college students with disabilities (Murphy, 1992).

Characterized by complex and often hidden impairments, students with learning disabilities contend with multiple challenges in accessing higher education, ranging from difficulty identifying their disability to obtaining appropriate accommodations. This chapter focuses on the role ADA plays in ensuring access and accommodation for students with learning disabilities at the postsecondary level. First, ADA will be reviewed and placed in a historical context; second, the concept of learning disabilities will be explicated; third, accommodations for learning disabilities at the postsecondary level will be examined in light of ADA requirements; fourth, two recent court cases will illustrate the impact of ADA on the provision of services to students with learning disabilites; and, finally, implications for the future of ADA and learning disabilities will be presented.

The Americans with Disabilities Act

Historically, individuals with disabilities have faced challenges restricting their access to private and public services, including transportation, employment, telecommunications, and education. These restrictions have often undermined the basic rights of individuals with disabilities, denying accessibility and usability of services most Americans take for granted. Over the last 25 years, new legislation has opened doors that were once closed to individuals with disabilities. In 1973, Section 504 of the Rehabilitation Act was enacted, banning discrimination against individuals with disabilities in institutions and programs receiving federal funds; in 1975 the Education for All Handicapped Children Act (now the Individuals with Disabilities Education Act) became law, ensuring a free appropriate public education for students with disabilities; more recently, ADA was passed. Signed into law in 1990, ADA ensures the rights of citizenship for individuals with disabilities by mandating the removal of barriers to complete participation in American society. Included in this mandate are protections that allow individuals to benefit fully from formal education without being penalized for a disability. This translates into "reasonable" accommodations for students with disabilities at postsecondary institutions, a factor that will be discussed later in this chapter.

As indicated above, the ADA augments the basic rights afforded by Section 504 of the Rehabilitation Act of 1973 (P.L. 93-112), which states: "No otherwise qualified handicapped individual in the United States, shall solely by reason of his handicap, be excluded or be denied the benefits of, or be subjected to discrimination under any program or activity receiving Federal financial assistance." This governing principle is reflected in ADA's purpose of ending discrimination against individuals in all facets of life.

ADA is comprised of five titles that enfranchise individuals with disabilities. Title I protects individuals from discrimination in employment; Title II addresses equitability in state and local government services; Title III ensures the provision of appropriate public accommodations by private entities; Title IV is concerned with accessibility of telecommunication services; and Title V covers miscellaneous provisions. These five titles serve to protect the individual with a disability across the spectrum of society. ADA defines the term "disability" as, "with respect to an individual, a physical or mental impairment that substantially limits one or more of the major life activities of such individual; a record of such impairment; or being regarded as having such an impairment."

Under the titles of ADA, students with disabilities have brought their case for "reasonable" accommodations to colleges and universities. Foremost among this group have been students with learning disabilities. In the next section the challenges faced by students with learning disabilities will be discussed.

Students with Learning Disabilities

The Individuals with Disabilities Education Act (1990) defines a learning disability as

a disorder in one or more of the basic psychological processes involved in understanding or in using language, spoken or written, which disorder may manifest itself in imperfect ability to listen, think, speak, read, write, spell, or do mathematical calculations.

Students identified with learning disabilities possess average to above average intelligence and usually demonstrate a significant discrepancy between aptitude and achievement as measured by selected standardized tests. By law, the primary cause of a disability may not be cultural, social, or environmental factors; nor visual, hearing or motor impairments; mental retardation or emotional disturbance.

Students with learning disabilities constitute a heterogeneous group (Mercer, 1997). Some may possess a specific disability in reading; others may have a disability in mathematics; still others may suffer from a more generalized impairment, such as listening, that will impact on all subjects requiring auditory processing of information. Because of the diversity among this group, it is difficult to describe the typical student with learning disabilities. While some researchers have noted some traits, such as attention problems, perception difficulties, memory problems, social – emotional problems, and motor disorders among certain groups of students with learning disabilities (Mercer, 1997), it is more beneficial to address each student's identified weakness individually when planning appropriate interventions.

The Challenge of Identifying a Learning Disability

Since 1975 when the federal government provided a definition, accurately identifying learning disabilities has been problematic. This is partly related to lack of clarity in the federal definition which governs the procedures in evaluating students for a disability (Brackett & McPherson, 1996; Hammill,1990; Keogh, 1983). Efforts to operationalize the definition by determining a "severe" discrepancy between potential and achievement have complicated the matter. Not everyone agrees on the numerical value of a severe discrepancy (Keogh, 1983; Mercer, Hughes, & Mercer, 1985). For example, when examiners compare a student's performance on two tests, one measuring potential and another achievement, there is no universal agreement on the number of points difference necessary to constitute a learning disability (Brackett & McPherson, 1996). Another issue is that of determining the "processes" contributing to the disability. Again, examiners do not share a common definition of processes, nor agree on which tests should be used to assess this construct, thereby making consistency in measurement difficult (Hammill, 1990; Adelman, 1992). Still another concern involves the requirement of ruling out contributing factors, such as cultural and environmental influences, that legally may not be the primary cause of a learning disability. Most everyone agrees it is difficult, if not impossible, to rule out those influences (Brackett & McPherson, 1996).

Ultimately, some students may be denied access to services because of inaccurate measurement procedures, while others may be misdiagnosed with a learning disability. This lack of consistency and questionable accuracy at the elementary and secondary school levels continue into the postsecondary level (Hoy, Gregg, Wisenbaker, Boham, King, Moreland, 1996; Ofiesh & McAfee, 2000), where examiners are equally perplexed about valid definitions and appropriate measurement tools. Thus, while ADA ensures access and accommodations for students with learning disabilities, problems with identifying who needs services may prevent many, otherwise eligible, students from ever realizing the benefits of the law.

The Growing Number of Students with Learning Disabilities on College Campuses

Over the past 25 years, the number of school students certified with learning disabilities has grown significantly. Today the category of learning disabilities constitutes more than 50% of the students with disabilities in the school system (U.S. Department of Education, 1997). At the postsecondary level a similar population boom is occurring among students with learning disabilities (Gregg & Scott, 2000; Vogel et al., 1999). This growth may be attributed to several factors. First, benefitting from effective interventions earlier in their lives, more students with learning disabilities are graduating from high school better prepared to continue their education. Second, supported by legislation, such as Section 504 and ADA, greater numbers of these students are gaining access to colleges and universities. Additionally, more college students are discovering they have learning disabilities for the first time. The late discovery of their disability may be related to the increased academic and organizational challenges of college life (Scott, 1997). Regardless of the reasons, these factors together contribute to a burgeoning population of students with learning disabilities on college campuses.

The large number of students with learning disabilities on college campuses means that institutions of higher education will have to expand their support services to remain in compliance with ADA. As cited in Harrison and Gilbert (1992), the law states:

No qualified individual with a disability shall, by reason of such disability, be excluded from participation in or be denied the benefits of the services, programs, or activities of a public entity, or be subjected to discrimination by any such entity.... No individual shall be discriminated against on the basis of disability in the full and equal enjoyment of the goods, services, facilities, privileges, advantages, or accommodations of any place of public accommodation by any person who owns, leases (or leases to) or operates a place of accommodation. (p. 162)

Thus, institutions of higher learning are charged with the responsibility of evaluating their programs, facilities, and services to determine areas of weaknesses, and then working to address those shortcomings. Where the institution falls short of providing reasonable accommodations, corrective action must be taken.

Accommodations for Students with Learning Disabilities

Depending on the student's disability, the accommodations will vary. "An accommodation does not guarantee success or a specific level of performance. It should, however, provide the opportunity for a person with a disability to participate in a situation or [an] activity." (Byrnes, 2000, p. 1). In essence, it should be "reasonable." Such accommodation may include:

(A) making existing facilities used by employees readily accessible to and usable by individuals with disabilities; and
(B) job restructuring, part-time or modified work schedules, reassignment to a vacant position, acquisition or modification of equipment or devices, appropriate adjustment or modifications of examinations, training materials or policies, the provision of qualified readers or interpreters, and other similar accommodations for individuals with disabilities. (Harrison & Gilbert, p. 91)

While virtually all colleges and universities have acknowledged the importance of providing equitable services to students with disabilities, it is fair to say that not all educational institutions have readily adapted to accommodate all students with disabilities, partly because of infrastructural challenges but perhaps mostly because of uncertainty about the extent of the law. Still, most colleges and universities can identify the necessary accommodations for students with obvious disabilities, for example, providing ramp access for individuals in wheelchairs. However, for individuals with an "invisible" challenge such as a learning disability, the necessary accommodations are not so readily apparent.

Indeed, one of the challenges students with learning disabilities face is convincing others of the existence of their disability (Stage & Milne, 1996); this is directly related to their ability to obtain appropriate accommodations. Even when documentation certifying their disability exists, getting others to understand the nature of their disability and its ramifications could be a formidable endeavor. Because a student's disability may be evidenced only when attempting certain activities, such as writing a paper or remaining focused during class lectures, their disability may appear nonexistent to others, or worse, as an excuse for poor scholarship. Ultimately, college faculty may minimize, if not ignore, their disability completely . Students, therefore, must take an active role in seeking and obtaining services. Unlike elementary and high school where much of what occurs in the provision of special services is determined by the school, at the college level it is the responsibility of the student to inform the institution of a disability and to request appropriate accommodations (Brinckerhoff, Shaw, & McGuire, 1992).

Types of Accommodations. Many types of accommodations exist. The student's specific learning disability must be considered when selecting what kinds of supports are suitable. The student and the institution work together to determine specific services and the most appropriate accommodations. To be effective any accommodation must be directly related to the identified disability. Every case is different and must be addressed individually. Some examples of accommodations include the following:

- *Extra time on tests and assignments.* Speed of processing may be a problem for many students with learning disabilities. Providing them with additional time may allow them to perform optimally without penalizing them for their disability.

- *Audiotaping class lectures.* Students with learning disabilities may have a fine motor skills deficit (causing handwriting difficulties) or an auditory processing weakness (affecting the ability to listen) that will prevent effective notetaking of lectures. Audiotaping would allow the students to replay lectures at a later time at their own pace.
- *Notetaker.* As stated above, fine motor skills deficits and auditory processing difficulties may affect the ability to take class lecture notes. A designated notetaker would assist students with learning disabilities in obtaining the needed information from lectures.
- *Course substitutions.* For some students with learning disabilities, learning a foreign language may be difficult. Where possible, allowing these students to substitute a course (e.g., a course on Spanish culture for a Spanish language course) may be appropriate.
- *Reader.* Many students with learning disabilities have deficits in reading. This makes it difficult for them to read their textbooks. Having someone read the textbooks to them would reduce the difficulty.
- *Books on tape.* As mentioned above, deficits in reading prevent many students with disabilities from reading the text. Books on tape allow these students to access the information in the textbooks.
- *Use of a computer word processor.* Students with learning disabilities who have handwriting difficulties benefit from a word processor. Also, students who have spelling weaknesses could use a spellchecker to assist them.
- *Alternative testing.* Tests requiring reading and writing may be difficult for students with learning disabilities. Allowing them to demonstrate their knowledge under a different format (e.g., an oral test) may improve their performance.
- *Testing in a separate environment.* For some students easy distraction presents a problem. To perform well these students need to be in an environment where they can remain focused. Allowing them to take a test individually in a separate room may alleviate the problem.
- *Alternative methods of instruction.* To assist students with learning disabilities, information should be presented in different modes, where possible. Some students with

learning disabilities may be more adept at grasping information presented visually than aurally. Using more graphics and other visual aids in instruction may enhance learning outcomes.

It should be noted that in accordance with ADA guidelines, the support provided to students should not compromise the basic integrity of a course, pose a threat to individual or public safety, or cause undue financial hardship on the institution. Accommodations, therefore, are not intended to provide the student with "an easy ride," nor are they designed to tax unconscionably the limited resources of an institution.

Whether or not a student is able to benefit optimally from accommodations may be dependent on the cooperation of the faculty member. Moreover, under the ADA, students and faculty "negotiate" accommodations (Scott, 1997), so that any modifications in the instructional program should be a mutual agreement. For the most part, research suggests that faculty are willing to provide accommodations where necessary to students with learning disabilities (Bourke, Streehorn, & Silver, 2000; Matthews, Anderson, & Skolnick, 1987; Nelson, Dodd, & Smith, 1991). Faculty tend to be more supportive of accommodations that are the least time-consuming (Vogel et al., 1999). Thus, faculty might be more willing to allow audiotaping of lectures than to prepare an alternative exam. The number of students in a class requiring accommodations could also pose an additional strain on a faculty member's time, resulting in resistance to provide these services (Bourke, Streehorn, & Silver, 2000). Still, the fact remains that the ADA requires institutions to provide reasonable accommodations, and the faculty, as agents of the institution, must be willing to negotiate such accommodations with students in good faith.

Two Court Cases Relying on the ADA

The ADA is an important legal defense tool in combating discrimination against students with disabilities. Recently, two prominent legal battles addressing the rights of students with learning disabilities have been decided. These cases help to illustrate the importance of the ADA in shaping policy and practices among institutions of higher learning.

In the first case, *Guckenberger v. Boston University* (1996), the issue of appropriate accommodations for students with learning disabilities was placed on trial. The legal dispute arose from a sudden change in university policy governing accommodations for students with learning disabilities. For years prior to its 1995 shift in policy, Boston University, under the coordination of its Learning Disabilities Support Services, provided accommodations to students with learning disabilities, including allowing the substitution of courses for foreign language and mathematics requirements. A review of this system, prompted by the provost of the university, resulted in a halt to the practice of substitutions and the posting of additional stipulations. Specifically, the new policy stated the following: (a) documentation of a disability must be no older than 3 years; students, moreover, would have to be retested every 3 years to retain eligibility for services; (b) course substitutions for mathematics and foreign language requirements would no longer be allowed; and (c) certification of learning disability would be accepted from only examiners with specific credentials (e.g., licensed psychologists). The new policy met with disapproval and resistance from students with learning disabilities, leading to a lawsuit against the institution. The students claimed that their rights, according to the ADA, Section 504, and the Massachusetts Constitution, were being violated.

In its decision the federal court found that the school's new policy did violate ADA as well as other laws. The court ruled against the 3-year retesting requirement, indicating that reassessment should be conducted only if specific situations warrant it. With regard to course substitution, the court decided that such an accommodation was legitimate, and that a course substitution for a foreign language was permissible. The university, however, was not ordered to waive the math requirement for the defendants since none of them had a math disability. As for the qualifications of evaluators, the court determined that a Ph.D. or M.D. was not required, provided the examiner possessed appropriate experience evaluating adults with learning disabilities. Thus, the decision of the court supported the rights of the students with disabilities

The second case, *United States of America v. National Collegiate Athletic Association* (1998), involved alleged discrimination against student athletes with learning disabilities by the National Collegiate Athletic Association (NCAA). The student athletes complained that the NCAA restricted their ability to play college sports and to receive athletic scholarships because of the NCAA's freshman eligibility policy. Under that policy, students aspiring to participate in Division I or II sports during their first year in college had to register with the NCAA and be certified. This allowed them to be eligible for an athletic scholarship from their selected college. Certification was granted based on four major criteria (Hishinuma, 1999):

- graduation from high school;
- successful completion (with at least a grade of D) of 13 core-curriculum academic courses;
- a GPA of at least 2.00 (higher, depending on SAT or ACT scores); and
- a combined score on the SAT verbal and math sections, or total score on the ACT, that met a "qualifier index" (p. 363).

A major concern for students with learning disabilities was that courses taught below the regular academic instructional level of the high school would not meet the 13-core curriculum requirement. This created a problem for students with learning disabilities since many of them had taken special education courses or had compensatory instruction. Another concern was the cutoff scores used for the ACT and the SAT, test measures that may not accurately reflect the true ability of students with learning disabilities.

The case was settled by consent decree. According to the agreement, the NCAA will modify its policies without compromising its academic standards. The NCAA will do the following: (a)revise their rules so that courses designed for students with learning disabilities will be certified as core courses, if the knowledge and skills provided in those courses are comparable to courses taken by students without disabilities; (b)allow students with learning disabilities who, as college freshmen, failed to meet the NCAA eligibility criteria to earn a fourth year of eligibility, if they are academically successful while participating in athletics; (c)consider several factors when deciding on a waiver; (d)include experts on learning disabilities on the Waiver Committees; and (e) appoint an ADA Compliance Coordinator for the NCAA.

Both of the cases discussed above suggest the power of ADA to move institutions towards equity in addressing the needs of students with learning disabilities. Whereas Boston University attempted to rescind accommodations afforded to their students with learning disabilities, the NCAA was unwilling to provide accommodations in their rules that would take into consideration the learning disabilities of students. Although the NCCA in its agreement never admitted it was in violation of ADA or even subject to it (Hishinuma, 1999), the fact that its amended rules attempted to meet the ADA mandate of reasonable accommodations indicated an improved awareness of equity for students with learning disabilities. These cases are only two examples of the struggle for access and accommodation in postsecondary education. Given the increasing number of students with learning disabilities seeking a college education, it is likely that more instances of disagreement between students and institutions will occur. Ultimately, students will seek redress under ADA, either inside or outside of court.

Implications

As the population of students with learning disabilities grows on college campuses, greater services and accommodations will be demanded. Most assuredly, students will utilize ADA to obtain the necessary institutional support for success. Institutions must prepare themselves to meet this challenge by (a)engaging in self-evaluation and monitoring, (b)educating administration, faculty, and staff, and (c)allocating the resources necessary to ensure access and accommodation for students with learning disabilities.

For institutions, self-evaluation of programs, services, and facilities is necessary to ensure compliance with ADA. This is best done under the guidance of a designated compliance officer of the institution who oversees the institution's efforts to meet the requirements of the law. A proactive approach to restructuring institutional policies and practices must be followed to allow for accessibility and accommodation. Moreover, self-monitoring must be practiced to identify weak areas, or those not in compliance with ADA regulations, and to make modifications when necessary.

Educating the administration, faculty, and staff about the provisions of ADA is certainly essential in building awareness of the rights of students with learning disabilities. It is important that service providers know the law if they are to adhere to it. It is equally important to sensitize university personnel to the challenges of students with learning disabilities. Understanding the difficulties these students face makes it easier to support them.

Finally, institutions must be willing to make an honest commitment to providing the resources necessary to support programs of access and accommodation. Just as resources will have to be expended for infrastructural changes to accommodate students with physical impairments (e.g., paraplegia), financial support will also be needed to provide tutorial services and counseling for students with learning disabilities. The establishment of a support center on campus that provides these special services and acts as an advocate for students with disabilities demonstrates an institution's commitment to this cause.

While the focus of this paper has been on one group of students with disabilities, institutions must provide equitable access and accommodation for all students with disabilities. Certainly, many of the accommodations noted for students with learning disabilities might apply to other disabilities as well (e.g., books on tape are important for students who are blind). Moreover, ADA mandates that facilities, services, and programs at colleges and universities accommodate all individuals with disabilities. Ten years after its enactment, ADA has proved to be an important milestone in the journey towards a society where disability is not a deterrent to full citizenship. For students with learning disabilities, it has made higher education a little more accessible and their difficulty in learning less of a deficit.

References

Adelman, H. S. (1992). LD: The next 25 years. *Journal of Learning Disabilities, 25*, 17-22.

Brackett, J., & McPherson, A. (1996). Learning disabilities diagnosis in postsecondary students: A comparison of discrepancy-based diagnostic models. In N.Gregg, C. Hoy, & A. Gay (Eds.), *Adults with learning disabilities: Theoretical and practical perspectives* (pp. 68-84). New York: Guilford Press.

Bourke, A. B., Strehorn, K.C., & Silver, P. (2000). Faculty members' provision of instructional accommodations to students with LD. *Journal of Learning Disabilities, 33* (1), 26-32.

Brinckerhoff, L. C., Shaw, S. F., & McGuire, J.M. (1992). Promoting access, accommodations, and independence for college students with learning disabilities. *Journal of Learning Disabilities, 25* (7), 417-429.

Byrnes, M. (2000). Accommodations for students with disabilities: Removing barriers to learning. *NAASP Bulletin, 84,* 21-27.

Gregg. N., & Scott, S. S.(2000). Definition and documentation: Theory, measurement, and the courts. *Journal of Learning Disabilities, 33* (1), 5-13.

Hammill, D.D. (1990). On defining learning disabilities: An emerging consensus. *Journal of Learning Disabilities, 23,* 74-84.

Harrison, M., & Gilbert, S. (Eds.) (1992). *The Americans with Disabilities Act Handbook.* Beverly Hills, CA: Excellent Books.

Hishinuma, E. S. (1999). An update on NCAA college freshman academic requirements: The impact on students with LD. *Journal of Learning Disabilities, 32* (4), 362-371.

Hoy, C., Gregg, N., Wisenbaker, J., Bonham, S.S., King, M., & Moreland, C. (1996). Clinical model versus discrepancy model in determining eligibility for learning disabilities services at a rehabilitation setting. In N. Gregg, C. Hoy, & A. F. Gay (Eds.), *Adults with learning disabilities: Theoretical and practical perspectives* (pp. 55-67). New York: Guilford Press.

Keogh, B. K. (1983). Classification, compliance, and confusion. *Journal of Learning Disabilities, 16,* 28-29.

Matthews, P., Anderson, D., & Skolnick, B. (1987). Faculty attitude toward accommodations for college students with learning disabilities. *Learning Disability Focus, 3* (1), 46-52.

Mercer, C.D. (1997). *Students with learning disabilities* (5th ed.). Upper Saddle River, New Jersey: Prentice-Hall, Inc.

Mercer, C. D., Hughes, C., & Mercer, A. R. (1985). Learning disabilities definitions used by state education departments. *Learning Disability Quarterly, 8,* 45-55.

Murphy, S.T. (1992). *On being L.D.: Perspectives and strategies of young adults.* New York: Teachers College Press.

Nelson, R., Dodd, H., & Smith, D. (1991). Faculty willingness to accommodate students with learning disabilities: A comparison among academic divisions. *Journal of Learning Disabilities, 23,* 185-189.

Ofiesh, N. S., & McAfee, J. K. (2000). Evaluation practice for college students with LD. *Journal of Learning Disabilities, 33* (1), 14-25.

Scott, S. S. (1997). Accommodating college students with learning disabilities: How much is enough? *Innovative Higher Education, 22* (2), 85-99.

Stage, F. K., & Milne, N. V. (1996). Invisible scholars: Students with learning disabilities. *The Journal of Higher Education, 67* (4).

U. S. Department of Education. (1997). To assure the free appropriate public education of all children with disabilities. *19ᵗʰ Annual report to Congress on the implementation of the Individuals with Disabilities Education Act.* Washington, DC: U.S. Government Printing Office.

Vogel, S. A., Leyser, Y., Wyland, S., & Brulle, A. (1999). Students with learning disabilities in higher education: Faculty attitude and practices. *Learning Disabilities Research & Practice, 14* (3), 173-186.

Table of Legal Cases

Americans with Disabilities Act, 1990, PL 101-336, 42 U.S.C. Sec. 12101.

Guckenberger v. Boston University, 974 F. Supp. 106 (D. Mass 1996).

Individuals with Disabilities Education Act of 1990, Public Law 101-476, 104 Stat. 1142 (1990).

Rehabilitation Act of 1973, Public Law 93-112, 87 Stat. 355 (1973).

United States of America v. National Collegiate Athletic Association. (Consent Decree, 1998). (See: http://www.usdoj.gov/crt/ada/ncaa.htm).

CHAPTER 5

PRIMING THE PUMP: MENTORING AND THE RETENTION OF AFRICAN AMERICAN FACULTY

Linda C. Tillman

At the beginning of a new century, the severe underrepresentation of African American faculty, and particularly in predominantly White institutions (PWIs), continues to be a concern. Recent statistics from the United States Department of Education indicate that in 1997 only 5% (27,723) of the total number of full time faculty positions (568,719) were held by African Americans (*Chronicle of Higher Education*, 2001). In addition, promotion and tenure rates for African Americans at all types of institutions in both the private and public sector rank among the lowest of all groups (Hutcheson, 1997). It is also more likely that African Americans will leave their positions before being promoted and tenured (Creamer, 1995).

Mentoring has been identified as a strategy to facilitate the professional growth and development of African American faculty and to increase their numbers in PWIs (Blackwell, 1988; Cartledge, Gardner, & Tillman, 1995; Frierson, 1998; Tillman, 1998; Tillman, 2001). Although mentoring has been hailed as an effective strategy for increasing the numbers of African American faculty, there are few empirical studies documented in the literature that have focused on mentoring as a strategy to address the retention of African Americans in PWIs. Clearly, there is a need for more in-depth investigations into ways that mentoring can be used as one strategy to increase the numbers of this group in PWIs.

This discussion is based on results from a study of ten African American faculty in two PWIs. Tillman (1995) identified five dimensions of faculty-to-faculty mentoring: mentor-protégé pairs, phases of the mentor-protégé relationship, mentor functions, benefits to the protégé, and race and gender in mentoring relationships. This discussion will focus on the mentor functions dimension – that is, how mentors helped to facilitate the professional and personal development of their protégés, and the implications for the retention of African American faculty.

Retaining African American Faculty

Given the underrepresentation of African Americans in higher education, the implementation of effective recruitment practices is an important factor in increasing their numbers as faculty members. However, it is equally important that once African Americans are hired, proactive strategies are implemented to maximize their opportunities for success (Cartledge, Gardner, & Tillman, 1995; Tillman, 2001). Professional and social isolation and a lack of scholarly productivity can contribute to a lack of success for some African American faculty in PWIs. Since African Americans are likely to be in departments and colleges where there are few, if any, faculty who share the same research, personal and cultural backgrounds, the opportunities to be selected as protégés may be limited. Because scholarly productivity is often tied to mentor relationships with senior faculty, majority faculty members should be encouraged to mentor and interact with minority faculty and to recognize and value different cultural backgrounds and scholarship which may be viewed as nontraditional. Mentors who are willing to socialize African American faculty to all of the aspects of the professoriate can play a critical role in increasing their promotion and tenure rates and retaining them in the institution. As Frierson (1998) has pointed out, mentoring does have an effect on professional success and advancement in the academic world.

In concert with an increased emphasis on mentoring as a retention strategy, a number of institutions have designed and implemented formal mentoring programs for under-represented groups. Boice (1992) found that minority faculty who participated in formal mentoring programs benefitted from the opportunity to analyze their accomplishments and to clarify the university's expectations for new faculty. However, Welch (1997) has cautioned that although more universities are implementing formal mentoring programs to assist underrepresented faculty, cross-race/cross-gender mentoring relationships for African Americans have met with limited success. Welch added that given this reality, planners should investigate what factors are critical to the development of effective comprehensive mentoring models for underrepresented groups. Such models should be designed and implemented to prepare faculty members to operate within the university setting, while also recognizing the individuality of faculty members' cultural backgrounds.

The preceding discussion challenges us to consider how institutions can address the issue of the retention of African American faculty. It is important that mentoring be considered as one method for enhancing their professional growth and development and increasing their numbers in PWIs.

Mentor Functions

Galbraith and Cohen (1995) describe mentoring as a process within a contextual setting; a relationship between a more knowledgeable individual and a less experienced individual; a means for professional networking, counseling, guiding, instructing, modeling, and sponsoring; a developmental mechanism (personal, professional, and psychological); a socialization and reciprocal relationship; and an opportunity for identity transformation for both the mentor and protégé. Mentoring has also been described as a communication relationship in which a senior person supports, tutors, guides and facilitates a junior person's career development, a relationship which is important in the academic world (Hill, Bahniuk, & Dobos, 1989).

Mentors can provide both career and psychosocial functions in faculty-to-faculty mentoring relationships (Jacobi, 1991; Noe, 1988; Tillman, 1998, 2001). Noe (1988) describes a number of related career and psychosocial functions which mentors may perform. Career functions prepare the protégé for career advancement and include protection (protection from committee assignments so that the junior faculty member's time is devoted to activities that are explicitly tied to achieving competence in research, teaching and service); coaching (providing direction about conceptualizing research questions and determining what are the most important questions to ask, inspiring self-confidence and encouragement, providing frank but confidential feedback, sharing ideas, and suggesting strategies for accomplishing specific academic tasks); and sponsorship (nominating the protégé for research projects, positions, and promotions, helping the protégé to secure needed resources and career enhancing opportunities, and assigning projects that increase the protégé's exposure and visibility to influential colleagues with similar research interests).

Psychosocial functions enhance the protégé's sense of competence, identity, and work-role effectiveness. These functions include role modeling (serving as an appropriate role model regarding attitudes, values, and behaviors); acceptance and confirmation (conveying unconditional positive regard for the protégé); and counseling (encouraging the protégé to talk openly about anxieties and concerns, and giving the protégé support that facilitates socialization and helps in coping with job stress and work demands of the new faculty role). Thus, the faculty mentor may perform a variety of functions which range from socializing the protégé to the organizational culture to providing emotional support. According to Noe (1988), the greater the number of career and psychosocial functions that are provided by the mentor, the more beneficial the relationship will be to the protégé.

Conceptual Framework

Mentor functions are an important and useful dimension of the conceptual framework for this study, and are used in the analysis and interpretation of mentoring experiences. In addition, the broad conceptual framework for this study is guided by the assumptions that mentoring is individualistic, may be different for African Americans, and can be used as a strategy to facilitate the professional growth, development, and retention of African American faculty in PWIs.

The findings in this study do not represent the complete range of possible mentoring relationships for African Americans in PWIs, and it is not the intent of this chapter to generalize the findings. However, the findings do provide insight into the effectiveness of mentoring as one strategy to address the issue of retention for this group.

Methodology

The purpose of this research was to investigate the mentoring experiences of African American faculty members in both formal and informal relationships in two predominantly White research institutions. A major focus of the study was how mentors helped protégés to prepare for the promotion and tenure review process. Mentoring the protégé for a successful promotion and tenure review is directly related to increasing diversity in higher education. The study was conducted at two large predominantly White research universities in the Midwest region of the country: University A, where faculty-to-faculty mentoring is accomplished through a *formal* (assigned) mentoring program, and University B, where faculty-to-faculty mentoring is accomplished *informally* by mutual consent. Nine untenured assistant professors (four females and five males) and one tenured associate professor (a male) and their mentors were interviewed regarding their mentoring experiences. Eight of the ten protégés had primary[1] mentors, and two protégés had both a primary mentor and a secondary[2] mentor.

Mentor-Protégé Relationships: Preparing the Untenured Faculty Member

Ideally, the greater the number of career and psychosocial functions that mentors perform, the more beneficial the relationship will be to the protégé. Although the number and type of functions varied, the majority of the mentors in this study did perform both career and psychosocial functions. Psychosocial functions included socializing with the protégés, providing encouragement, and counseling protégés about job related stresses and managing faculty demands. Career functions included socializing protégés to the departmental and institutional norms, nominating them for awards, introducing them to influential persons, and collaborating with them on research and publications. The most important career function that mentors performed was helping protégés to meet the specific requirements for promotion and tenure.

The majority of the protégés in this study indicated that their mentors performed career functions which were critical to their professional growth and development, and which would ideally help them to be promoted and tenured. A female protégé in an informal relationship made a direct link between mentoring and the career functions her mentor performed. She explains in the following statement:

> If a mentor is mentoring, there's a change in your professional development. It affects how you develop professionally.

Given the imperative to research and publish in predominantly White research institutions, mentors and protégés placed a great deal of emphasis on research and writing. A key factor related to the emphasis on research and writing was starting early. In most cases in this study, mentors began to provide assistance during the protégé's first year. For example, two males, one in an informal mentoring arrangement, and one in a formal mentoring arrangement had mentors who, during their first year, helped them to map a strategy for meeting the research and publishing demands of their institutions. For both new faculty members, this plan included setting goals for the number of publications needed for the promotion and tenure review. Their mentors also assisted them by helping them to conceptualize their research, helping them to identify and gain access to research sites, reading and critiquing drafts of manuscripts, socializing them to the publication process, helping them to identify publication outlets, and collaborating with them on research and writing projects. Both protégés indicated that they understood the importance of getting started early or 'hitting the ground running' as critical to being prepared for a successful promotion and tenure review. The following statement is illustrative of this point:

> I think it would be difficult without a mentor because when you come into the academy there are no clear cut standards. Nobody says, if you get five articles published in referred journals, you will be tenured and promoted. It's not that cut and dry. No one tells you that if you teach effectively, you will get it either. It's just nebulous and therefore you need somebody to tell you that you are going in the right direction.

Both of these protégés had impressive publication records, had received awards for teaching and service, and were granted promotion and tenure. Thus, in these two cases long-term, consistent career mentoring which began early in their careers was a key factor.

Long-term, consistent mentoring was not the case for all of the protégés in this study. A female protégé in an informal mentoring arrangement was "informally assigned" a mentor in her fourth year. Rather than providing her with career and psychosocial functions throughout her probationary period, it was only during the last two years of her probationary period that her mentor assisted her in the areas of research and writing – areas which were most important to the protégé at the time. The mentor performed functions which were in direct response to the protégé's need to improve her publication record so that she could be promoted and tenured and remain in the institution. When asked if their mentoring arrangement had been a successful one, the mentor replied, "It will be if she gets tenure." The protégé was promoted and tenured and did remain at institution. However, she felt that she would have benefitted more from a long-term, consistent mentoring arrangement (beginning in her first year) focused on helping her to establish a publication record which was acceptable to the department, college, and the institution.

The majority of the protégés in this study placed more emphasis on career functions that their primary mentors performed than on psychosocial functions. Eight of the untenured faculty members had cross-race mentors (seven white and one Latina). Findings from this study indicate that African American protégés may seek out same-race mentors to provide them with psychosocial support to combat feelings of loneliness and isolation in PWIs. Several protégés indicated that they had experienced feelings of isolation and that at times they felt they might have to compromise their cultural identity to fit into their institution. A male protégé elaborated on this point in the following statement:

> There are times when I still feel alone. There are times when I still feel that even though I'm able to interact and intermingle in the culture, that I'm clearly not under-stood. That's probably where someone like my second-ary mentor comes in, or some of my other colleagues at other universities who are African Americans.

Like the protégés, the majority of the White mentors in this study also placed less importance on performing psychosocial functions. These mentors indicated that they were not as comfortable providing their protégés with functions such as emotional support and role modeling and indicated that this was, to a great extent, based on cultural differences. For example, most of the White mentors felt that they could provide career functions such as coaching and sponsorship, but named another African American as the person whom their protégé would probably identify as their role model or counselor. A mentor emphasized this point in the following statement:

> The demography of the institution is terrible. This is not a place for minorities to feel very comfortable or have very many minority colleagues. I think they (other African American faculty) would be good role models, and I think it would daily reinforce the notion that Black people have tenure, they have a voice, they have succeeded. These may be in some small way, role models to my protégé which say, yes there are some successful Blacks on the faculty.

These findings lend support to Thomas's (1990) argument that same-race mentor-protégé relationships provide significantly more psychosocial support than cross-race relationships, and that African Americans have a need to form both organizational and developmental mentoring relationships. These organizational and developmental relationships can help to reduce the sense of isolation that the protégé alluded to in his statement. Thus, it is both the professional (career) and personal (psychosocial) support that is provided by mentors that can be factors in protégés success and their decision to remain in the institution.

The majority of the protégés indicated that their mentors provided them with career guidance that helped them to grow as professionals; nevertheless, protégés did make a distinction between the career and psychosocial functions their mentors performed, a distinction that was based on the race of the mentors. While the literature does not adequately describe the linkages between the types of functions that mentors perform and the race match of mentor-protégé pairs, both protégés and mentors in this study did make such race-function distinctions in a consistent pattern.

Mentor Functions: Benefits to the Protégé

Professional and personal benefits can accrue to the protégé faculty member as a result of a successful mentoring relationship. Findings in this study indicate that the benefits to the protégé can be linked to the functions that their mentors performed. Eight of the nine untenured faculty members in this study were promoted and tenured and remained in their institutions. In most of the cases, the extent to which protégés benefitted from the mentoring relationship appeared to be related to the career functions that mentors performed which resulted in their being promoted and tenured. Mentors worked closely with their protégés to make sure they understood the expectations of the tenure review committee at the departmental and divisional levels, gave them advice about where they should put more or less emphasis in their research, and kept them informed about their chances for being granted promotion and tenure. Since the purpose of the formal mentoring program at University B was to provide protégés with a series of structured activities which would prepare them for a favorable promotion and tenure review, a great deal of the formal mentoring was focused on providing the protégé assistance in the areas of research and publication.

Ideally, planned and structured mentoring experiences are more beneficial to the protégé. But the type of mentoring arrangement (planned mentoring experiences versus informal mentoring experiences) were not significant factors in this study. Protégés in informal mentoring relationships were as productive as those in formal mentoring relationships. Thus, in most cases in this study the perceived success of the mentoring relationship was linked to the benefit of being promoted and tenured.

Hill, Bahniuk, and Dobos (1989) have noted that mentoring does not determine the success of the protégé, but rather success is multi-faceted and is dependent on many variables. The terms *success* (benefits) and *successful mentoring relationship* were defined by the participants. Because of the small sample, no definite conclusions can be made about the links between success and mentoring. But based on interviews with the participants, it is clear that to some degree, protégés and mentors in this study equated career success with being promoted and tenured and remaining in their position in their institution. For example, when protégés and mentors were asked, "Do you believe it is important for faculty members to have a mentor?" the majority of them replied "yes" and went on to elaborate that it is very difficult for untenured junior faculty to experience career success without a mentor. A protégé elaborated on this point in the following statement:

> I think it would be difficult without a mentor. You need someone to guide you. A mentor is someone who gives you critical feedback, support and encouragement. The mentor provides opportunities for you to try some things on your own with the knowledge that you can come back, bounce ideas, bounce questions, talk about failures as well as successes.

Nevertheless, no claims can be made that a successful mentoring relationship as described in the literature or by participants in this study is the only reason that a faculty member is promoted and tenured. There are a number of other factors which may also affect this critical aspect of the faculty member's career. Thus, it is not an assumption of this study that protégés experience career success and/or are promoted and tenured solely on the basis of successful mentoring relationships.

The Imperative for Retaining African American Faculty: Implications for Practice

Mentoring was successful for the majority of the untenured faculty in this study. Eight of the untenured protégés were promoted and tenured. While there was no overwhelming evidence to support formal over informal mentoring arrangements, most of the protégés felt that institutions should implement support systems for new untenured faculty. This point is significant since African American faculty are often caught in a 'revolving door' syndrome (Blackwell, 1988), in which they are retained for five or six years, evaluated negatively for tenure, and are then required to leave the institution. In addition, Judson (1999) reports that African American faculty often do not have a clear understanding about retention and the promotion and tenure process (how their scholarship will be evaluated). A support system which is designed to assist protégés over the duration of their untenured status can help to reverse the revolving door syndrome. The reversal of this revolving door syndrome can positively impact the retention of African American faculty. Moreover, mentoring programs should be designed and implemented with the specific context of the institution in mind. As Welch (1997) has noted, such initiatives should be implemented after consideration of the university setting and the faculty members' cultural backgrounds. Institutions must do more than just recruit African American faculty – they must also assume responsibility for implementing polices and practices that will help increase the number of African American faculty who are promoted, tenured, and retained in PWIs.

A major finding in this study related to mentor functions was that both protégés and mentors placed more emphasis on career functions than they did on psychosocial functions. When implementing mentoring programs, department chairpersons and/or program planners must determine which career and psychosocial functions are most important and should consider not only the expectations of the department, but also the professional and personal needs of new untenured faculty members. Given the culture of major research institutions, being granted promotion and tenure is likely to be one of the most effective ways to retain African American faculty. Thus, ongoing communication between department chairpersons, and mentors and protégés is important. The implementation of activities which are specifically designed to assist protégés in meeting the requirements for promotion and tenure should be the focus of many of the functions.

An additional finding in this study which related to mentor functions was that the majority of the protégés separated the functions that their mentors performed based on the race of the mentor. These protégés relied on their African American secondary mentors or other African Americans (inside and outside of their institutions) to provide them with psychosocial support. Thus, efforts should be made to identify senior African American faculty (both inside and outside of the institution) who are willing to serve as mentors. Professional organizations, support groups, and contact with other institutions that have successfully identified senior African American faculty can all be valuable sources of information. The additional effort can be a determining factor in the protégé's success and his or her decision to remain in the institution.

The professional and social isolation of African American faculty was a significant issue for the majority of the protégés in this study. The culture of the department and the institution is central to the issue of retention. Is the culture of the institution and the department accepting and inclusive? Or, like some of the protégés in this study, do African American faculty feel that they "do not belong" or that they must compromise their identity and their scholarship to "fit in"? Department chairpersons can play a key role in assuring that the culture of the department is one where the contributions of all faculty members are valued and where there is a commitment to the success of every faculty member.

The findings discussed here point to issues of access and equity for African American faculty, and particularly those in PWIs. Mentoring should be considered as one strategy to assure that new faculty achieve maximum professional and personal success and that they are retained in the institution. However, more must be done to assure that the professoriate is an accessible and equitable profession. Institutions must be proactive in the recruitment, hiring, and retention of African American faculty.

Notes

1. The individual whom the protégé identified as that person who consistently engaged in mentoring activities. All of the primary mentors were employed at the same university as the protégés. Noe (1988) defines primary mentoring relationships as those which provide the complete range of career and psychosocial functions.
2. The individual whom the protégé identified as that person who engaged in mentoring activities, but to a lesser extent. All of the secondary mentors were employed at the same university as their protégés. The term secondary mentor as used in this study is not intended to mean that this individual performed mentoring functions in the absence of the primary mentor. Rather some protégés had more than one mentor and this term was used to make a distinction between the mentors.

References

Blackwell, J. (1988). Faculty issues: The impact on minorities. *The Review of Higher Education 11*(4), 417-434.

Boice, R. (1992, Summer). Lessons learned about mentoring. *New Directions for Teaching and Learning 50*, 51-61.

Cartledge, G., Gardner, R., & Tillman, L. (1995). African Americans in higher education special education: Issues in recruitment and retention. *Teacher Education and Special Education 18*(3), 166-178.

Creamer, E.G. (1995). The scholarly productivity of women academics. *Initiatives 57*(1), 1-9.

Employees in Colleges and Universities by Racial and Ethnic Group, Fall 1997 (2001). *Chronicle of Higher Education Almanac*.

Frierson, H.T. (ed.) (1998). *Diversity in Higher Education: Examining Protégé-Mentor Experiences.* Vol. I & II. Stamford, CT: JAI Press, Inc.

Galbraith, M.W. & Cohen, N.H. (eds.) (1995). *New Strategies and Challenges.* San Francisco: Jossey Bass Publishers.

Hill, S.E., Bahniuk, M.H., & Dobos, J. (1989). The impact of mentoring and collegial support on faculty success: An analysis of support behavior, information adequacy, and communication apprehension. *Communication Education 38*(1), 15-33.

Holland, G. (1998). The mentoring of faculty and administrators in higher education. In H.T. Frierson (ed.). *Diversity in Higher Education: Examining Protégé-Mentor Experiences.* Vol. II, pp. 7-40. Stamford, CT: JAI Press, Inc.

Hutcheson, P.H. (1997). The corrosion of tenure: A bibliography. *The NEA Higher Education Journal 13*(2), 89-106.

Jacobi, M. (1991). Mentoring and undergraduate academic success: A literature review. *Review of Educational Research 61*(4), 505-532.

Judson, H. (1999). A Meaningful Contribution. In W.B. Harvey (ed.). *Grass roots and Glass ceilings: African American administrators in predominantly White colleges and universities.* pp. 83-111. Albany, NY: State University of New York Press.

Noe, R. A. (1988). An investigation of the determinants of successful assigned mentoring relationships. *Personnel Psychology 41*(3), 457-479.

Thomas, D.A. (1990). The impact of race on managers' experiences of (mentoring and sponsorship): An intra-organizational study. *Journal of Organizational Behavior 11*(6), 479-492.

Tillman, L. (2001). Mentoring African American faculty in predominantly White institutions. *Research in Higher Education(42)*3, 295-325.

Tillman, L. (1998). Mentoring of African American faculty: Scaling the promotion and tenure mountain. In H.T. Frierson (ed.). *Diversity in Higher Education: Examining protégé-mentor experiences*, Vol. II, pp. 141-156. Stamford, CT: JAI Press, Inc.

Welch, O. (1997). An examination of effective mentoring models in academe. In H.T. Frierson (ed.). *Diversity in Higher Education: Examining Protégé-Mentor Experiences*, Vol. I, pp. 41-62. Stamford, CT: JAI Press, Inc.

SECTION II.

The Policy Context

CHAPTER 6

STATE TAX EFFORT AND FEDERAL FINANCING OF HIGHER EDUCATION: UNCOMMON AGENDAS AND FISCAL PRACTICES

F. King Alexander

The purpose of this chapter is to argue that federal higher education funding and policies ignore disparities in state fiscal capacity and effort, both vital and pivotal aspects of any definition of an equitable system[1]. The federal government perversely provides relatively more funding to institutions in those states that have greater fiscal capacity and exert less tax effort to support public higher education. In other words, it appears that the result of the overall federal policy is to reward richer states for the lack of tax effort for public higher education.[2] However, before discussing the role of the federal government in addressing disparities in state tax effort and spending for higher education, it is important to analyze the disparate willingness of states to support higher education and various institutional sectors.

In Adam Smith's first of four "canons" of taxation, he stated that

> the subjects of every state ought to contribute towards the support of government, as nearly as possible, in proportion to their respective abilities; that is, in proportion to the revenue which they respectively enjoy under the protection of the state. (Smith, p. 355)[3]

105

Smith's statement reflects the need for governments to adopt progressive taxation policies that do not disproportionately burden lower socioeconomic populations. Smith also advances the concept that taxation for government services should not be assessed and measured independently from the wealth of a state's citizenry. Thus, it is insufficient for governments to invest in human capital without accounting for wealth because richer governments putting forth the same tax effort as poorer governments will always appear to be making a greater fiscal effort.

Using tax effort to adjust for wealth is particularly relevant when comparing how governments invest in human capital through education. Education constitutes a significant portion of most state budgets while also providing some of the greatest individual and social returns to state citizens. The causal-effect relationship of education and development is self-evident and now indisputable, with the contribution of higher education integral to the creation and dissemination of essential knowledge. Numerous studies have shown that the rates of return to investment in higher education continue to be significant for individuals and society (McMahon, 1999; see also, Becker, 1993; Leslie & Brinkman, 1993; Paulsen, 1994). Thus, an important task of policy-makers is to ensure that investment in higher education is adequate and equitable.

When making public investment determinations, conducting comparative studies regarding how states invest and use their fiscal capacity to support higher education is helpful. This study was devised to compare the willingness of states to invest in higher education and the various institutional sectors. By comparing current state expenditures and fiscal tax effort for higher education, the data presented in this study shed some light on the various fiscal strategies employed by states in supporting the various higher education sectors, and, in doing so, reveal any disparities and inequities that exist among the states.

State Tax Effort Comparisons

For purposes of determining equity, interstate comparisons are useful in measuring the level of fiscal condition of education in and among states. According to Halstead, "the common identity which States must share in order to be compared is usually similar socioeconomic characteristics and organization" (Halstead, 1975, pp. 46-47). Halstead further added that to conduct comparative studies between states, it is possible to group states by similarity of (1) basic socioeconomic strength to support [higher] education, (2) manner of organizing for education, or (3) emphases on educational components. This study focuses on the first of Halstead's premises, measuring the basic socioeconomic strength of a state to support higher education. Using accurate socioeconomic measurements to assess changes in a state's commitment to higher education is a common practice that is frequently used by policymakers and other governing officials.

One of the most important indicators used to compare and monitor changes in national, state, and local investment for higher education is tax effort. Information concerning the ability of governments to obtain resources for public purposes and the extent to which these resources are used enables officials to more accurately determine the value of existing fiscal practices.

The tax effort of a government to support higher education is influenced by many historical, socioeconomic, and political factors. Examples of some forces which shape higher education include, the people's interest and attitude toward different higher education sectors; the proportion of students enrolled in each sector; the people's attitude about government and taxes; the amount of taxes citizens pay for programs other than higher education; and, the fiscal capacity of a state or the people to support public investment in higher education. The effect of any one of these factors, or any combination of factors, by a state to invest in higher education has always been difficult to determine. However, it is generally accepted that each of these factors play an important role in allocating public resources to higher education students and institutions.

Tax effort is defined as the extent to which a government uses its fiscal or tax capacity to support higher education (Alexander & Salmon, 1995). It can also be characterized as the level of taxpayer exertion made to fund a specific government service. By measuring the tax effort of a state to expend public resources for higher education, we are able to avoid problematic comparisons in state spending in simple dollar terms, because wealthier states have larger actual increases in aggregate and per student spending. Moreover, the use of tax effort allows policymakers to more accurately determine how economically disadvantaged states invest in higher education and other government services when compared to more economically advantaged states. When the fiscal capacity of a state to support higher education and other government services is not taken into account, which is frequently the case, aggregate and per student state/local expenditures usually show that wealthier states appear more committed to higher education and many other public services. Thus, it is important when determining relationships between expenditures and revenues, to account for variations in the overall fiscal capacity of governments and people to support these social enterprises.

State governments, more than any other single element in American society, have assumed the responsibility of financing public higher education. States together with local governments, provided over $60.6 billion in state tax funds for higher education in 2000-2001.[4] This constitutes nearly 40% of the revenue received by all higher education institutions received in 2000-2001 (Mortenson, 2000). For most public colleges and universities, state governments are the largest single source of revenue for annual operating expenses. This high degree of reliance on state governments places public institutions in a precarious environment that is significantly impacted by economic and political fluctuations in fiscal support as witnessed in the 1980s and 1990s (see also Griswold & Marine, 1998; Hines, 1988). Also, although higher education has become nearly a universal necessity for states, it remains a discretionary part of state budgets making it extremely vulnerable to economic and ideological policy changes (St. John, 1994). As states are the primary source of revenue for the vast majority of public institutions (enrolling approximately 75% of all higher education students), it is surprising that relatively little attention has been given at the federal level to the considerable differences in state expenditures and tax effort among states for supporting higher education.

Previous research on state tax effort has primarily focused on declining trends in fiscal support for higher education by states during the last three decades (Mortenson, 2001). The findings presented from most of these analyses have been used to make ominous predictions about the future of state support for higher education. The most widely accepted approach to determining the level of tax effort that states exert to support higher education is measured by examining spending per student relative to per capita personal income to the resident (Lieberman, 1998). By calculating the percentage of per capita personal income that is spent on higher education for each student, state tax effort can be determined and regularly compared with other states. Personal income provides an approximate measure of the capacity of state residents to pay taxes for higher education and other government services.

This study embraces a commonly used tax effort measurement to compare the fiscal effort or tax effort of states to one another.[5] This method analyzes tax effort by comparing state higher education expenditures per full time equivalent (FTE) student. Using this technique permits a tax effort analysis by a commonly accepted variable that takes into account important enrollment differences between states and institutional sectors. Another popular tax effort technique used by Halstead and Mortenson compares state investments for higher education by determining each resident's fiscal contribution to higher education per $1,000 of personal income. This method is used to conduct state tax effort comparisons in annual reports highlighted in *The Grapevine* and *Postsecondary Education Opportunity* (Hines & Palmer, 1988; Mortenson, 2000). State tax effort per $1,000 of personal income will only be briefly alluded to in this paper.

In this study, state tax effort for higher education spending by sector and per student is measured by combining state appropriations for operating expenses, local appropriations for operating expenses, and state student aid appropriations. Local appropriations are allocated to higher education institutions in only twenty-five states, while state student aid appropriations are annually appropriated in nearly every state. Once aggregate state expenditures have been determined, state spending per FTE student by sector are calculated and adjusted to compensate for average state income disparities.[6] Then the states are ranked by their ability and willingness to support varying higher education sectors.

State Tax Effort for Higher Education

The vast majority of annual state spending for higher education emanates from three primary sources; state appropriations, local appropriations, and student aid appropriation. State appropriations provide the lion's share of government revenues to colleges and universities; local appropriations to public community colleges constituted over $4.5 billion in twenty-five states in 2000-2001; and, state student aid appropriations reached nearly $4 billion in 2000. Due to a variety of factors briefly discussed earlier in the paper, substantial disparities exist in state higher education investment. For example, state spending per FTE student for all higher education in the lowest ten expenditure states constituted only 54 percent of the national average in state higher education spending in 2000-2001. Many of the nation's wealthiest states fall far below the national effort average in exertion of tax effort for supporting higher education. As Figure 1 indicates, states that are found in the upper and lower right quadrants are wealthy states that differ drastically in their support for higher education. Of the 23 states located in the upper and lower right quadrants only California, Wisconsin, New Jersey, Hawaii, Florida, Nevada, Michigan, Oregon, and Nebraska exert more tax effort for higher education than the national average. The willingness of some of these states to support higher education is demonstrated in Table 1 as an indexed listing of high and low tax effort states.

Table 1. Tax Effort by States in All Higher Education

High Tax Effort States		Low Tax Effort States	
New Mexico	183.5%	Vermont	17.9%
Mississippi	175.9%	New Hamp.	31.9%
Arkansas	165.5%	Maine	43.2%
Wyoming	148.6%	Rhode Island	46.7%
Kentucky	141.6%	Massachusetts	48.2%
Idaho	136.7%	Colorado	50.6%
Alabama	135.9%	New York	54.5%
Hawaii	135.2%	Alaska	59.9%
California	132.7%	Pennsylvania	66.9%
Oklahoma	124.4%	West Virginia	74.4%
Kansas	123.9%	South Dakota	75.5%
Nebraska	121.7%	Connecticut	79%
Arizona	120.8%	Ohio	84.4%
Wisconsin	118.8%	Delaware	85.8%
North Carolina	117.4%	Montana	88.4%
US. Average	100%		

Figure 1 illustrates that the states in the lower right quadrant are wealthy states that have low tax effort for higher education. The states located in the upper left quadrant are relatively poor states that invest heavily in higher education. The bottom left quadrant identifies states that are relatively poor and do not invest very much in higher education.

Figure 1. State Tax Effort per FTE for all Higher Education, 2000 - 2001.

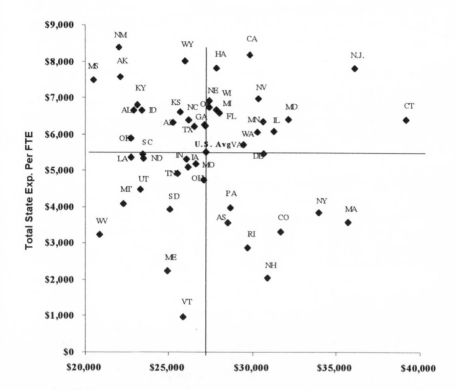

As Figure 1 shows, generally, in the northeast region of the United States, where public spending for higher education has traditionally been comparatively low, only New Jersey appears to exert enough tax effort for higher education to rank above the national tax effort average. Although Connecticut has above average higher education expenditures per FTE, its tax effort is substantially below the national average due the state's very high wealth. Outside the northeastern corridor of the United States, other wealthy states also exert tax effort far below the national average including Colorado, Virginia, and Illinois.

On the other hand, many of the poorer states including New Mexico, Mississippi, Arkansas, Wyoming, and Kentucky are among the nation's leaders in tax effort per FTE for higher education. For example, Kentucky and Colorado are states that have comparable FTE student populations, yet Kentucky exerts over two and a half times more tax effort than does than Colorado for higher education. Kentucky also has much higher tax effort for higher education than all its neighboring states including Tennessee, West Virginia, Indiana, Ohio, and Illinois.

State Tax Effort for Public Four-Year Universities

When assessing state tax effort for higher education by institutional sector, significant differences emerge in the way states choose to finance higher education opportunities. Many states advance differing philosophies regarding support for one or another institutional sector. In most cases, states prioritize one of the three primary institutional sectors, public 4-year universities, public two-year colleges, private 4-year colleges and universities. In rare instances, all three institutional sectors are equally supported by the state. To understand better how states support different higher education sectors, this section of the paper will analyze state tax effort by each institutional sector.

In every state, public four-year universities receive the largest total amount of public funding for higher education. However, state support per student for public four-year universities varies considerably. State spending for public four-year universities ranges from $14,851 per FTE student in Hawaii to $2,219 per FTE student in Maine. As Figure 2 shows, the national average for state spending per FTE student for public universities in $8,279. North Dakota, Alabama, Michigan, and Oregon are states that fund their public universities nearest to the national average. When comparing state tax effort for public universities, numerous states appear to be significantly investing in their public four-year sector while other states do very little for their public four-year universities. As shown in Figure 2, states in the upper right and left quadrant are spending at levels above the national average. Some of these states are also exerting significant tax effort in support of their public universities.

Figure 2. State Tax Effort per FTE for Public Four-Year Universities, 2000 - 2001.

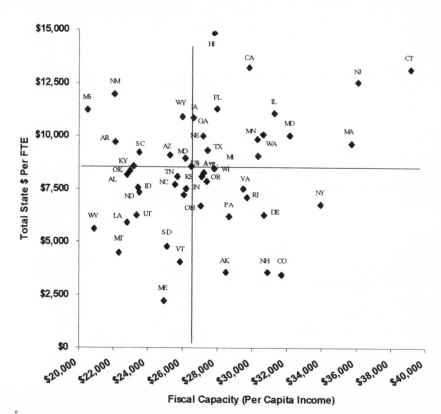

Fiscal Capacity (Per Capita Income)

States located in the upper left quadrant of Figure 2 including New Mexico, Mississippi, Arkansas, Wyoming, Kentucky, and South Carolina are among the nation's leaders in their willingness to fund public universities. A number of wealthy states in the upper right quadrant including California, Hawaii, Florida, Iowa, and Illinois are also funding their public universities at levels greater than the national average. States that exert the lowest tax effort in their funding of public universities are found in the lower right and left quadrants. Many of nation's more affluent states are found in the lower right quadrant where state willingness to support public universities is comparatively low, including Colorado, New York, Pennsylvania, and Virginia. The willingness of some of these states to support public four-year universities is shown in Table 2 in an indexed listing of high and low tax effort states.

Table 2. Tax Effort in Public Four-Year Universities.

High Tax Effort States		Low Tax Effort States	
Mississippi	177.9%	Maine	28.9%
New Mexico	176.2%	Colorado	35.6%
Hawaii	176.5%	New Hamp.	37.6%
California	144.2%	Alaska	40.7%
Arkansas	142.8%	Vermont	51.1%
Wyoming	136.6%	South Dakota	61.7%
Iowa	132.8%	New York	64.8%
Florida	130.7%	Montana	65.3%
South Carolina	127.7%	Delaware	66.5%
Kentucky	120.6%	Pennsylvania	70.6%
Georgia	119.7%	Rhode Island	77.7%
Alabama	118.7%	Ohio	80.3%
Arizona	116.9%	Virginia	82.8%
Oklahoma	116.8%	Louisiana	84.3%
Illinois	115.5%	Utah	86.8%
U.S. Average	100%		

State Tax Effort for Public Two-Year Institutions

Public two-year institutions generate revenues from all three government sources analyzed in this study. State appropriations for operating expenses, local appropriations, and state student aid assistance provide the majority of public two-year institution funding. State appropriations account for the lion's share of public two-year institution funding; over $4.5 billion is allocated to two-year institutions in twenty-five states from local appropriations. By receiving annual support from multiple funding sources, it should not be surprising that vast disparities exist in state expenditures per student and tax effort for public two-year colleges. In fact, through the use of these multiple funding sources many states including Colorado, Maine, and New Hampshire, provide more state support per FTE student to public community colleges than they expend for public universities. It is also important to note that state spending per student for two-year public colleges in nine states exceeds public university expenditures per student in New York, Ohio, Pennsylvania, and Louisiana.

When comparing state expenditures and willingness to support two-year public colleges, two interesting findings emerge. First, tax effort for public two-year universities varies considerably. State spending for public two-year universities ranges from over $8,000 per FTE student in Maine, North Carolina, and Wisconsin to under $3,000 per FTE student in Georgia, North Dakota and South Carolina. As Figure 3 shows, the national average for state spending per FTE student for two-year public colleges is $5,129, approximately 39% below state expenditures per FTE for public universities. States that expend resources for two-year public colleges nearest the national average include Arizona, Hawaii, Texas, Alabama, Colorado, Pennsylvania, Illinois, and Virginia.

Second, when analyzing state tax effort for two-year public colleges numerous states appear to be significantly investing in their public two-year sector while other states do very little for their public colleges. In Figure 3, states in the upper right and left quadrant are spending at levels above the national average. Many of these states are also exerting significant tax effort in supporting their public two-year campuses. States exerting high tax effort are in the found upper left quadrant of Figure 3 including North Carolina, Maine, Kentucky, Oregon, and Louisiana. Numerous wealthy states exert significant tax effort for two-year public colleges as shown in the upper right quadrant including California, Delaware, Massachusetts, Wisconsin, Nebraska, and Michigan. States that exert the lowest tax effort for two-year public colleges are found in the lower right and left quadrants.

Several states exerting the lowest tax effort for two-year public colleges are identified in the lower right and left quadrants of Figure 3. In the lower right quadrant many wealthy states which exert little fiscal support are shown including Maryland, Colorado, Florida, New Hampshire, and Ohio. The lower left quadrant shows the poorer states that also refuse to exert less than average tax effort for public two-year campuses. The willingness of some of these states to support two-year public higher education is shown in Table 3 (which follows Figure 3) in the indexed listing of high and low tax effort states.

Figure 3. State Tax Effort per FTE for Public Two Year Institutions, 2000-2001.

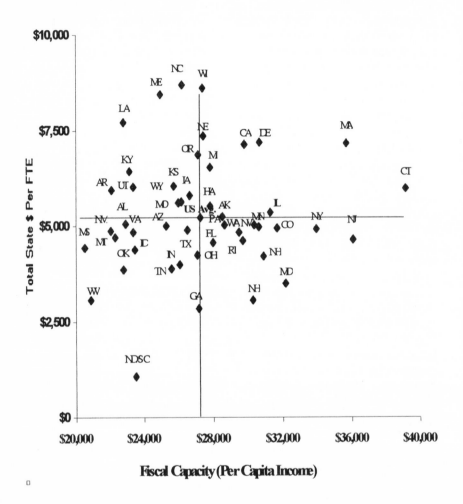

Fiscal Capacity (Per Capita Income)

Table 3. Tax Efforts by State in Public Two-Year Colleges

Highest Tax Effort States		Lowest Tax Effort States	
Maine	175.6%	Vermont/S.D.	0%
Louisiana	175.6%	South Carolina	23.6%
North Carolina	172.1%	North Dakota	23.7%
Wisconsin	163.2%	Georgia	54.1%
Kentucky	144%	Maryland	56.4%
Arkansas	139.5%	New Jersey	67%
Nebraska	139.4%	New Hampshire	70.8%
Utah	133.6%	New York	75.4%
Oregon	131.3%	West Virginia	76.1%
California	124.6%	Tennessee	79%
Delaware	122%	Connecticut	79.5%
Michigan	121.8%	Indiana	79.8%
Kansas	118%	Rhode Island	80.1%
Iowa	117%	Colorado	81.4%
New Mexico	117.5%	Ohio	81.6%
U.S. Average	100%		

State Tax Effort for Private Four-Year Institutions

Since the passage of the Higher Education Act of 1965 and the subsequent federal amendments of 1972, private higher education institutions in the United States have increased their reliance on federal and state resources primarily through direct student aid programs.[7] After nearly three decades of growth and expansion of direct student aid funding at the state level, state financing of private colleges and universities has become an important and increasingly controversial issue for policy-makers. Currently, nearly $2 billion annually is allocated to private institutions by state legislatures.

However, despite the consistent growth in public assistance to private campuses, state support for private higher education varies considerably from state to state. Generally, states where private colleges and universities have experienced a long historical presence, as they do in many of the old Colonial states, state funding for private higher education has always been part of the financial landscape. In other states and regions of the country such as the most western and southern states, very little interest in funding private higher education has been expressed by state legislatures. These historical developments have led to vast disparities in state expenditures per student and tax effort for private colleges and universities in the United States. Currently, state funding per FTE student for private institutions varies from $2,079 in New Jersey to $0 in Alaska, Wyoming, South Dakota, and Nevada.

When comparing state expenditures and willingness to support private higher education, wealthy states appear to fund their private higher education sector at greater levels than do poorer states. According to Figure 4, states allocating the largest amount of funds per student for private higher education are found primarily in the upper right quadrant. Many poorer states have also begun to support private higher education institutions but expend considerably less per student than their wealthier counterparts. Several of these states can be identified in the upper left quadrant of Figure 4.

The data presented in this study also indicate that some states such as Florida, New Jersey, Michigan, Illinois, and Iowa exert over twice the national average tax effort for private higher education. However, many other states primarily located in the Far West, and in some cases, the South, exert far less tax effort for private higher education than do their more affluent northern neighbors. The willingness of some of these states to support private higher education is shown in the indexed listing of high and low tax effort states.

Figure 4.   State Tax Effort per FTE for Private Four Year
Universities, 2000-2001.

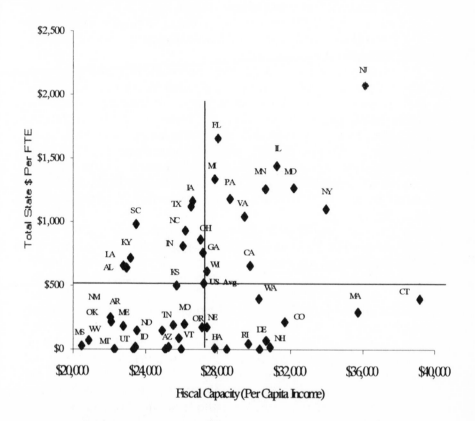

Table 4. Tax Effort by State in Private Four-Year Institutions.

Highest Tax Effort States		Lowest Tax Effort States	
Florida	272.9%	Alaska, South Dakota, Wyoming, & Nevada	0%
New Jersey	266.5%	Montana	.35%
Michigan	221.6%	Utah	.7%
Illinois	213.2%	Hawaii	1%
Iowa	208.7%	Arizona	2.32%
Texas	195.5%	New Hampshire	3%
South Carolina	193.2%	Idaho	3.43%
Pennsylvania	190.5%	Mississippi	6.7%
Minnesota	190%	Rhode Island	6.7%
Maryland	182%	Delaware	9.8%
North Carolina	164%	West Virginia	14.5%
Virginia	164%	Vermont	15.9%
New York	150%	Maine	27.9%
Ohio	146.7%	Oregon	28.9%
Indiana	143.5%	Nebraska	28.9%
U.S. Average	100%		

The Federal Government and State Tax Effort Disparities

The disparities in state expenditures per student and in state tax effort raise concerns regarding the role of states and the federal government in financing higher education. Since the Constitution makes no special reference to education, assumptions are made that education is the legal and primary responsibility of the states. However, the federal government is not prohibited from providing federal assistance to states or educational institutions. History is replete with examples of federal legislation that has aided schools, colleges, and universities. In fact, many of the nation's most innovative educational experiments were initiated by the federal government such as the Morrill Acts, the Smith-Level Act, the G.I. Bill, and Title I and II, ESEA legislation.

Recently, some education experts have called for expansion of the federal role in education. However, most of the attention encompassing an increase in federal involvement has occurred in the K-12 arena (see Wise, 1990; Lu, 1991). Any previous expansion of the federal government's role in education, at any level, was usually desired by those who believe that only by the infusion of federal funds or fiscal incentives can equalization among states be achieved. A federal effort to achieve a national level of financial support for all higher education students has been deemed consistent with other efforts to equalize educational opportunities at all levels. According to the National Education Association, "anything less than interstate equalization leaves students and parents in some states at a disadvantage."(National Education Association, 1993, p. 30).

Under current federal higher education policy, little is done to address the tax effort disparities among the states highlighted in this chapter. In fact, over three decades of federal direct student aid policies, and most recently, tax credit and deduction federal legislation, have simply advanced a "one size fits all" federal agenda ignoring the distinctive institutional interests and missions of public, private, and proprietary institutions. In establishing federal tax credits and deductions for higher education costs and expenses, students and institutions were granted comparable benefits regardless of state investment disparities or institutional missions. On the other hand, federal direct student aid policies have exacerbated inequalities between states because funds are disproportionately awarded to students attending higher cost institutions (Alexander, 1998). States that do not restrict their public colleges and universities from increasing their reliance on tuition-based revenues are more likely to benefit disproportionately from federal direct student aid funds. States that maintain a low tuition philosophy regarding their public higher education institutions, generally, are less likely to see their students proportionately benefit from direct student aid policies. The states that maintain low tuition strategies are primarily poorer Southern and Western states with relatively low per capita personal incomes by national standards. Many wealthier states, primarily in the Northeast and Midwest, have the luxury to utilize higher tuition strategies that indirectly benefit their institutions with greater federal assistance. For high-tuition private institutions and other public universities that have tuition autonomy, the federal policies of the last three decades have proven extremely lucrative.

However, as previously shown, not all wealthy states have high fiscal tax effort for public higher education. Many wealthy states, primarily located in the northeast region of the country, advance high tuition/high aid fiscal strategies for their public campuses while investing comparatively little public resources directly to their public colleges and universities. New York, Maine, New Hampshire, Vermont, and Massachusetts expend comparatively little resources on students attending public campuses, but these same states that are among the nation's leaders when allocating public resources to private college and university students.

If the federal government were to attempt to address higher education expenditure and tax effort disparities between states, it should recognize two important factors. First, any federal plan should acknowledge the importance of investment in students and higher education institutions and confirm that adequate state investment in human capital is in the national interest. Such a plan should advance the value of human capital and knowledge-based investment in higher education and call for investment strategies at the state and national level in keeping with that foundational objective. Second, the plan should be funded by the federal government at a level sufficient to maintain a competitive standard of federal funding and to provide an impetus for states to fund their higher education institutions more adequately. Any federal plan should provide fiscal incentives that reward states for maintaining "above average" tax effort in investing in higher education opportunities and institutions. States that would benefit from such an initiative include many poorer states such as Alabama, New Mexico, Mississippi, Kentucky, Wyoming, and Arkansas. Also, many wealthier states such as California, Hawaii, New Jersey, Wisconsin and Michigan would also benefit from the federal assistance due to their relatively high fiscal support of higher education. Under such a plan, states that opt to invest below the national average or below their fiscal capacity would not receive federal assistance. This federal initiative would serve as an economic disincentive against maintaining low public support for higher education. States that would currently be negatively impacted include many wealthy states that provide comparatively little effort for public higher education such as New York, Virginia, Ohio, Massachusetts, Connecticut, Colorado, and Washington. Poorer states that also would be negatively impacted by such a plan include West Virginia, Montana, Tennessee, and Utah because they refuse to provide adequate investment for higher education despite having a higher fiscal capacity to do so.

Conclusion

The findings presented in this chapter advance a number of important issues for policy-makers and higher education officials. First, significant disparities continue to persist in the way that states finance higher education systems and sectors. Second, regardless of their limited wealth, poorer states tend to exert more tax effort in supporting public higher education, while wealthier states are unwilling to support public higher education adequately. Third, wealthier states, generally, exert more tax effort for private higher education than do poorer states. Fourth, states exerting high tax effort for public higher education also are less reliant on tuition revenues while many wealthy states, which exert low tax effort for public higher education, usually rely heavily of tuition-based revenues and have higher student costs.

These findings raise serious concerns regarding the funding strategies and fiscal inequalities that exist in higher education in the United States. The substantial disparities in state per student expenditures and tax effort shown above, demonstrate the severity of these inequalities resulting in drastic fluctuations in higher education opportunities for students and families throughout the nation. The willingness, or lack of willingness, of states to support higher education at adequate funding levels shows the understated significance of state residency in the United States. These fiscal disparities in state tax effort also demonstrate a need for the federal government to develop policies that do not exacerbate current disparities among states. By taking into account state fiscal capacity and effort, the federal government could develop a new higher education policy that would provide economic incentives to ensure that all states provide adequate and consistent investment for higher education. A federal policy of this kind could provide important resources that could better stabilize the highly volatile environment of state financing for higher education.

Notes

1. I would like to thank Jeff Cross, Associate Vice President for Academic Affairs, Eastern Illinois University and Zhaohui Wang, Graduate Assistant, Department of Educational Organization and Leadership, University of Illinois at Urbana-Champaign for their assistance in the paper.
2. A preferred method of measuring state tax capacity is a system developed by the Advisory Commission on Intergovernmental Relations (ACIR) called the "representative tax system" (RTS). "The RTS estimates the amount of revenues that each state government, with its local governments, could derive from imposing, at average rates, a standard tax system made up of the various taxes and quasi-taxes that are actually levied by states and local governments." See: Advisory Commission on Intergovernmental Relations, *1988 State Fiscal Capacity and Effort* (Washington, D.D.: ACIR, August 1990), M-170, p.3. Also see K. Halstead, *State Profiles: Financing Public Higher Education 1978 to 1994*, (Washington, D.C.: Research Associates of Washington, 1994), p. 47.
3. Aggregate state appropriations include state appropriations for operating expenses, local appropriations, and state direct student aid assistance
4. The tax effort calculation is defined as "the ratio of revenue (or expenditure) to the tax base." Personal Income or the Representative Tax System (RTS) are the most commonly used methods to determine the tax base of states. See: K. Alexander and

R. Salmon, *Public School Finance* (Boston: Allyn and Bacon, 1995), p. 174. Halstead extends the tax effort measurement to what he calls "overall state and Family Funding Effort" in which he includes a combined set of inputs and output factors that incorporate not only tax effort, but a tuition factor as well. See Halstead, p. 54.

5. State per capita personal income data is provided by The Bureau of Economic Analysis

6. It is also important to note the significance of the U.S. Supreme Court decision in *Tilton v. Richardson* in 1971. This ruling upheld the Higher Education Facilities Act of 1963 which allowed for the allocation of public resources for facility construction at private colleges and universities. The *Tilton* case set off a wave of federal legislation where the Supreme Court upheld publicly aiding private higher education institutions while striking down similar programs aiding primary and secondary education. Once the legal barriers were cleared at the federal and state levels, state legislatures quickly enacted a series of direct student aid policies that providing public assistance to private colleges and universities.

References

Alexander, F.K. (1998). Private institutions and public dollars: An analysis of the effects of direct student aid on Public and private institutions of higher education. *The Journal of Education Finance, 23*(3), 390-417.

Alexander, K. & Salmon, R. G. (1995). *Public School Finance.* Boston: Allyn and Bacon.

Becker, G. S. (1993). *Human Capital.* Chicago: University of Chicago Press.

Fair Chance Act, Subcommittee on Elementary, Secondary, and Vocational Education of the House Committee on Education and Labor, The. 101st Congress, 2d Sess. (1990) (testimony of A. Wise).

Griswold, C. P. & Marine, G. M. (1998). Political influences on state tuition-aid policy: high tuition/high aid and the real world *Research in Higher Education, 35* (1), 311-329.

Halstead, K. (1975). *Statewide Planning in Higher Education.* Washington, DC: U.S. Department of Health, Education, and Welfare.

Hines, E. R. (1988). *Higher Education and State Governments: Renewed Partnerships, Cooperation, or Competition?* (ASHE-ERIC Higher Education Report No. 5). Washington D.C.: Association for the Study of Higher Education.

Hines, E.R. & Palmer, J. (2000-2001). *The Grapevine.* Raw data.

Leslie, L. & Brinkman, P. (1993). *The Economic Value of Higher Education.* Phoenix: Oryx Press.

Lieberman, C. (1998). *Educational Expenditures and Economic Growth in the American State.* Akron, OH: Midwest Press.

Lu, C. P. (1991). "Liberator or captor: Defining the role of the federal government in school finance reform," *Harvard Journal on Legislation 28*, (2), p. 543-564.

McMahon, W. W. (1999). *Education and Development: Measuring the Social Benefits.* Oxford: Oxford University Press.

Mortenson, T. (2000). *Postsecondary Education Opportunity.* Okaloosa, Iowa: November, Number 100.

Mortenson, T. (2001). *Postsecondary Education Opportunity.* Okaloosa, Iowa: November, Number 112.

National Education Association, (1993). *What Everyone Should Know About Financing Our Schools.* Washington, D.C.: NEA.

Paulsen, M. B. (April, 1994). *The Effects of Higher Education on Workforce Productivity in the Fifty States.* Paper presented at the annual meeting of the American Educational Research Association. New Orleans, Louisiana.

Smith,A. (1776). *The Wealth of Nations,* Book. V, Chapter 3, p.355.

St. John, E. P. (1994). *Prices, Productivity, and Investment: Assessing Financial Strategies in Higher Education.* (ASHE-ERIC Higher Education Reports No. 3). Washington, D.C.: Association for the Study of Higher Education.

CHAPTER 7

DIVERSITY MEETS ADVERSITY: NATIONAL LEGAL BACKLASH TO HIGHER EDUCATION AFFIRMATIVE ACTION PROGRAMS

Kristine K. Otto

The debate around minority-designated scholarships is delicate and explosive, because it affects so deeply the lives of those students concerned and because it exists in the nebulous region between affirmative action and reverse discrimination.
                                          Barry, 1992, p. 6

The answer to the "delicate and explosive" question of whether it is legal to award scholarships based on race is one which varies from state to state across the United States. The unsettled nature of this legal question makes it very difficult for public colleges and universities to be confident that the diversity and affirmative action policies that they fashion with the best of intentions will withstand the toughest legal scrutiny. Indeed, "the use of race as a reparational device risks perpetuating the very race-consciousness such a remedy purports to overcome" (*Maryland Troopers Association v. Evans*, 1993). How much of this risk should a university take, knowing that challenges to affirmative action will not cease in the foreseeable future? "Affirmative action as a national policy is . . . one whose importance will dominate public [debate] well into the [twenty-first] century" (Hendrickson, 1996, p. 351).

Adversity to universities' affirmative action and diversity efforts is evident in the way in which affirmative action law is changing across the U.S. In fact, "many Americans are uncomfortable about the use of race as a factor in admitting students to selective colleges and professional schools" and "critics have attacked the policies on several grounds" (Bowen and Bok, 1998, p. xxiii). As a result, many public institutions of higher education have found themselves named as defendants in lawsuits regarding their student admissions and scholarship funding policies and practices.

Outcomes of this litigation have, in recent years, not been favorable for universities' affirmative action efforts. As a result, at some institutions, affirmative action in admissions (*Hopwood v. State of Texas,* 1996) or scholarship programs (*Podberesky v. Kirwan,* 1994/1995) has been eliminated, or admissions or scholarship criteria have changed. For example, the University of Massachusetts at Amherst limited its use of race in admissions in order to avoid lawsuits that have challenged affirmative-action policies like those in Michigan and Texas (Selingo, Jan. 21, 2000). Enough disparity is present in litigation, voter initiatives, and public opinion to suggest that "the controversy is moving toward some new authoritative review and resolution" (Bowen and Bok, 1998, p. 14). In order to understand the debate more fully, a summary of the 2000 U.S. legal climate is provided here, followed by a look at the University of Texas' alternate undergraduate admissions and scholarship model, established in response to a court decision that forbade its law school's challenged practices.

Title VI and the Fourteenth Amendment

Racial discrimination litigation usually alleges that a process violates both Title VI of the Civil Rights Act of 1964 ("Title VI") and the equal protection clause of the Fourteenth Amendment to the U.S. Constitution. Title VI prohibits discrimination in programs receiving federal financial assistance, and states:

> No person in the United States shall, on the grounds of race, color, or national origin, be excluded from participation in, or be denied the benefits of, or be subject to discrimination under any program or activity receiving

Federal financial assistance (Civil Rights Act of 1964, Pub. L. No. 88-352, 78 Stat. 241).

Title VI's implementing regulations state that a funding recipient (such as a university) "must take affirmative action to overcome the effects of prior discrimination" if the recipient has previously discriminated (34 C.F.R. 100.3 (b)(6)(i)).

The equal protection clause of the Fourteenth Amendment guarantees equal protection under the law and states, in pertinent part: "No State shall . . . deny to any person within its jurisdiction the equal protection of the laws." The application of this clause to higher education was tested in the 1978 Supreme Court decision *Regents of the University of California v. Bakke*, discussed below.

Although at first blush it seems that any form of racial discrimination is, without exception, invalid, this analysis is untrue. Not all classifications based on race are illegal. Certain race-conscious remedial measures may be upheld as constitutional if they satisfy both prongs of a two-part analysis, known as "strict scrutiny." The measures taken must: (1) serve a "compelling governmental interest," and (2) be "narrowly tailored" to achieve the goal in question. The concepts of "compelling governmental interest" and whether race-conscious remedial measures are "narrowly tailored" were illuminated with respect to higher education in the 1978 Supreme Court decision *Regents of the University of California v. Bakke*.

Tension between Court Decisions
Regents of the University of California v. Bakke (1978)

In *Regents of the University of California v. Bakke* (1978), a White applicant to the University of California-Davis Medical School, Allan Bakke, challenged the university's admissions programs as violating both the Fourteenth Amendment and Title VI. The school had both a "regular" admissions program and a "special" admissions program, each administered by a separate committee. The special admissions program – for educationally or economically disadvantaged applicants – operated as a quota to admit sixteen members of minority groups to the medical school each year. Candidates in this special admissions program did not have to meet the 2.5 GPA cutoff of the regular admissions program, and were not compared with candidates in the regular admissions program. No disadvantaged Whites had ever been admitted under the special admissions program, although many were eligible to apply and had done so (*Regents of the University of California v. Bakke*, 1978).

Bakke, twice rejected under the regular admissions program, alleged that the special admissions program operated to exclude him unlawfully on the basis of his race. The University of California did not deny that it operated two programs, and offered four justifications for classifying individuals on the basis of race in its special admissions program. The four proffered justifications for the special admissions program were:

> (i) reducing the historic deficit of traditionally disfavored minorities in medical schools and in the medical profession . . . ;
> (ii) countering the effects of societal discrimination . . . ;
> (iii) increasing the number of physicians who will practice in communities currently underserved; and
> (iv) obtaining the educational benefits that flow from an ethnically diverse student body (*Regents of the University of California v. Bakke*, 1978, p. 306).

The U.S. Supreme Court, in applying a strict scrutiny analysis to the program, examined the four proffered justifications to determine which, if any, of them served a "compelling governmental interest" – that is, which were substantial enough to support the University's decision to make distinctions among applicants based on their races. The concept of strict scrutiny stems from the idea that "racial and ethnic distinctions of any sort are inherently *suspect* and thus call for the most exacting judicial examination" (*Regents of the University of California v. Bakke*, 1978, p. 291) (emphasis added). Strict scrutiny dictates that a classification based on, for example, race, meet a compelling governmental interest and be narrowly tailored to achieve the stated, legitimate goal. A compelling governmental interest could be established through a judicial, administrative, or legislative review that found evidence of past discrimination at the specific institution in question, not in society in general (*Regents of the University of California v. Bakke*, 1978). Narrow tailoring means that the program that serves the compelling governmental interest must be designed to incur the least possible amount of harm on others. The Supreme Court, in carrying out its strict scrutiny analysis, then examined the four proffered purposes to decide which, if any, of them served a compelling governmental interest – that is, which were substantial enough to justify the university's use of the suspect classification of race. The Court said that the first three of the four reasons offered were invalid, and held that the special admissions program violated both Title VI and the Fourteenth Amendment (*Regents v. Bakke*, 1978).

The Court's reasoning for finding each of the first three justifications invalid follows. As to the first justification, the Court said that this preferential purpose was facially invalid. "Preferring members of any one group for no reason other than race or ethnic origin is discrimination for its own sake. This the Constitution forbids" (*Regents v. Bakke*, 1978, p. 307). With respect to the second justification, the Court said that it was invalid because a state may not prefer members of one group over another in order to remedy "societal discrimination," which is "an amorphous concept of injury that may be ageless in its reach into the past" (*Regents v. Bakke*, 1978, p. 367). Had there been a judicial, legislative, or administrative finding of constitutional or statutory violations (in which a judicial, legislative, or administrative body defines the extent of the injury and the consequent remedy), the result may have been different. Such a finding would justify aiding individuals of victimized groups at the expense of innocent individuals. The line of reasoning here is that the legal rights of the injured must be vindicated; therefore, a substantial, or compelling, interest exists in preferring them over members of other groups. The "remedial action usually remains subject to continuing oversight to assure that it will work the least harm possible to other innocent persons competing for the benefit" (*Regents v. Bakke*, 1978, p. 308). No such judicial, legislative, or administrative findings of past discrimination, however, are present in this case. The Court found the third proffered justification invalid because there was no evidence in the record, save a newspaper article, to show that the special admissions program was needed to promote the goal of improving health-care delivery to underserved communities.

Although it held the first three justifications invalid, the Court did not hold outright that the fourth was invalid, and seemed to accept it by saying that the concept of educational diversity could serve as a compelling interest to justify race-conscious affirmative action (*Regents v. Bakke*, 1978). The Court's analysis of reason (iv) included the statement that "the interest of diversity is *compelling* in the context of a university's admissions program" (*Regents v. Bakke*, 1978, p. 314), (emphasis added). In addition, the Court said that the attainment of a diverse student body "clearly is a constitutionally permissible goal for an institution of higher education" (*Regents v. Bakke*, 1978, p. 312). Furthermore, the Court said that "academic freedom, though not a specifically enumerated constitutional right, long has been viewed as a special concern of the First Amendment. The freedom of a university to make its own judgments as to education includes the selection of its student body" (*Regents v. Bakke*, 1978, p. 312).

In a valid affirmative action admissions program, the Court said, race may be used as one of a number of factors, but not the sole factor, in the higher education admissions process. To this day, many colleges and universities employ this rationale in their admissions processes, using race as one of many factors in admissions decisions in order to achieve diverse classes (Bowen and Bok, 1998).

Hopwood v. State of Texas (1996)

Although *Regents of the Univ. of Cal. v. Bakke* is a Supreme Court decision, and, in theory, its holding should apply across the U.S., three states (Louisiana, Mississippi, and Texas) do not abide by its ruling due to the controversial 1996 *Hopwood v. State of Texas* decision in the Fifth Circuit. The facts in *Hopwood v. State of Texas* (1996) are similar to those in *Regents v. Bakke* (1978), in that a graduate school specializing in professional education employed an admissions system that considered applicants' races; in both cases, denied White applicants sued. The *Hopwood v. State of Texas* plaintiffs alleged that The University of Texas Law School's two-track admissions system gave substantial racial preferences to African Americans and Mexican Americans in an effort to meet a 5% and 10% class composition of these groups, respectively (*Hopwood v. State of Texas*, 1996). Four White Texas residents who were denied admission sued, alleging violations of the Fourteenth Amendment and Title VI (*Hopwood v. State of Texas*, 1996).

In this case, interestingly, the Fifth Circuit put forth a holding contrary to *Regents v. Bakke* (1978), barring any consideration of race in the higher education admissions process (unless necessary to remedy past discrimination by the University of Texas Law School itself). In effect, this ruling proclaims dead (at least in the Fifth Circuit states of Louisiana, Mississippi, and Texas) the Supreme Court's earlier "educational diversity" justification for validly taking race into account in the admissions process, as was held in *Regents v. Bakke* (1978). The Fifth Circuit stated that the "educational diversity" justification presented in *Regents v. Bakke* did not rise to the level of a compelling governmental interest, and therefore the Law School's admissions process did not begin to meet the first prong of the strict scrutiny analysis described earlier. Upon appeal, the Supreme Court denied *certiorari*, thereby failing to issue clear guidance in this area. On remand from the Fifth Circuit, the district court determined that each plaintiff was entitled to $1 in damages (*Hopwood v. State of Texas,* 1998).

The discrepancy between these two rulings has resulted in confusion for higher education admissions professionals at public institutions across the country for many reasons. First, there is tension between the laws. The lower Fifth Circuit has, in effect, invalidated a ruling of the highest court in the land – the U.S. Supreme Court. Although the Fifth Circuit's decision applies in only three states, could a similar decision occur in another circuit? Second, it seems that the legal recommendation is easy if the institution is not located in Louisiana, Mississippi, or Texas – follow *Regents v. Bakke* (1978), and, with the goal of educational diversity, consider race as one of many factors in the admissions process. However, the situation becomes complicated when it is discovered that well-intentioned universities in states outside the Fifth Circuit are being slapped with "reverse discrimination" lawsuits. Third, how does the law apply in areas related to admissions, but outside of the admissions process, for example, in the realm of scholarships for minority students? Minority student funding programs have not yet been tested at the Supreme Court level, but have been tested at the Circuit Court level, in *Podberesky v. Kirwan* (1994/1995).

Podberesky v. Kirwan (1994/1995)

The Court of Appeals for the Fourth Circuit[1] struck down a race-specific scholarship program at the University of Maryland-College Park (UMCP) in 1994. In this case, UMCP's Benjamin Banneker scholarship program was at issue. The Banneker program was a merit-based program open only to African American students. Podberesky, a Caucasian and Hispanic student, met all other requirements for this program, but was ineligible to apply for a Banneker award because of his race. UMCP had another scholarship program that was not designed exclusively for African Americans, the Francis Scott Key program, but Podberesky's academic credentials were insufficient to be competitive in this program. The University of Maryland, in defending its program, presented four distinct "present effects of past discrimination" that it claimed the Banneker program was designed to remedy (*Podberesky v. Kirwan*, 1994, p. 153). The four present effects of past discrimination that UMCP proffered were:

- UMCP's poor reputation in the African American community;
- underrepresentation of African American students at UMCP;
- low retention and graduation rates for African American students; and,
- perception of the campus climate as racially hostile (*Podberesky v. Kirwan*, 1994/1995).

However, the Fourth Circuit, applying a strict scrutiny analysis, said that none of these four effects were sufficient to justify the Banneker program, as none satisfied the two-part test established by the court to determine whether a compelling governmental interest was present. In order to satisfy this test, the university needed to show that the present effects of past discrimination were: (1) caused by past discrimination,[2] and (2) of sufficient magnitude to justify the program. In carrying out the full strict scrutiny analysis mentioned earlier, however, the court reasoned that even if the two-pronged compelling governmental interest test were satisfied, the program was not narrowly tailored to achieve the overall goal of the program. The case was appealed to the Supreme Court, but, like *Hopwood v. State of Texas* (1996), the Court denied *certiorari*. As a result of the Fourth Circuit decision, the Banneker program at UMCP has been combined with the Francis Scott Key program, and criteria for the new single program include "diversity, special talents/skills, extracurricular involvement, essay, recommendations, high school performance, and test scores" (Clague, 1996, p. 33).

Pending Cases in Michigan and Washington

Although court decisions such as the ones described above provide today's legal guidance, current litigation in Michigan and Washington reveal upcoming trends and may provide a glimpse into the future. In theory, the Supreme Court eventually could rule on one of these extant controversies to provide a final answer to the question of using race in the higher education admissions process. It is interesting to note that in all three cases described below, the Center for Individual Rights (CIR) is representing the plaintiffs free of charge, as it does for all of its clients (T.J. Pell, personal communication, June 12, 2000). CIR is a non-profit public interest law firm based in Washington, D.C., and also represented the *Hopwood v. State of Texas* (1996) plaintiffs free of charge. CIR's stated purpose is to defend individual rights, especially in the areas of civil rights, freedom of speech, the free exercise of religion, and sexual harassment (CIR Home Page, 2000). This legal group interprets Title VI and the Fourteenth Amendment strictly, to say that government should never distinguish among people based on their races.

Michigan
Currently, the University of Michigan is a defendant in two admissions lawsuits, one against its undergraduate school and one against its law school. The undergraduate suit is known as *Gratz v. Bollinger, et al.* (1997) and the law school suit as *Grutter v. Bollinger, et al.* (1997). Both suits were filed in 1997 in the federal court for the Eastern District of Michigan in Detroit (Fact Sheet, 2000).

The cases remain separate, although there are many similarities between the two. Plaintiffs in both cases, all of whom are White, were denied admission to the university – Jennifer Gratz (Fall Term 1995) and Patrick Hamacher (Fall Term 1997), who applied for admission to the College of Literature, Science, and the Arts, and Barbara Grutter (Fall Term 1997), who applied for admission to the Law School. Both cases have been certified as class actions, and, in them, plaintiffs allege that the university unlawfully takes race into account in its admissions process, violating Title VI and the Equal Protection Clause of the Fourteenth Amendment (*Grutter v. Bollinger, et al. and Gratz v. Bollinger, et al.,* 1999). The university's response is that indeed it does take race into account, but does so lawfully, relying on the Supreme Court standard set forth in *Regents v. Bakke* (1978), that the educational benefits yielded from diversity constitute a compelling governmental interest for justifying its narrowly tailored admissions procedures (Information on Admissions Lawsuits, 2000).

Another similarity between these two cases is that intervention of student and citizen groups has been permitted in each (*Grutter v. Bollinger, et al.* and *Gratz v. Bollinger, et al.,* 1999). These intervenors will be defending the University's racial-consideration policy on the theory that it is "needed to remedy past and/or present discrimination against minorities" (Fact Sheet, 2000). The two cases are, however, scheduled for trial at different times: *Gratz v. Bollinger, et al.* in late 2000, and *Grutter v. Bollinger, et al.* in 2001 (Law school admissions trial suit delayed, 2000).

Washington

Another pending case on the topic of student admissions is *Smith v. University of Washington Law School* (1999). Like the Michigan cases just described, this case was filed in 1997. The district court denied summary judgment in 1999, and the case continues to be litigated. The issue in this case is similar to the cases just discussed – whether a university's admissions system unlawfully discriminated against an applicant on the basis of her race.

Katuria Smith, a White applicant, was denied admission to the 1994 entering class of the University of Washington Law School (UWLS). She alleges that UWLS used different admissions standards for different applicants, based on race (Center for Individual Rights, 1997). Now a graduate of Seattle University School of Law's class of 1997, she seeks monetary damages from being forced to attend a less prestigious, more expensive school

(Foster and Schubert, 1998). UWLS, like the University of Michigan in *Gratz v. Bollinger, et al.* and *Grutter v. Bollinger, et al.*, acknowledges that it considered race in its admissions process ("Numbers Bind," 1998). Like the *Hopwood v. State of Texas* (1996) case, however, Smith says that educational diversity is not a compelling governmental interest that justifies this race-conscious admissions program. A federal district court judge held in 1998 that Washington's voter passage of Initiative 200[3] that same year made much of the case moot. This judge also held that *Regents v. Bakke* (1978) would be controlling law. Plaintiffs appealed these rulings to the Ninth Circuit Court of Appeals; the Circuit Court affirmed the lower court's decision (Hebel, 2000).

Because the case law in the area of affirmative action in higher education admissions is unsettled, it is important to monitor any development very closely. The Michigan cases have the most potential for appeal to the Supreme Court level.

Federal Agencies, Policies, and Programs

Office for Civil Rights of the U.S. Department of Education
In addition to case law, other components of the federal environment must be explored in this analysis. The U.S. Department of Education's Office for Civil Rights (OCR) has been involved with affirmative action in the form of higher education desegregation since 1969,[4] which marked the beginning of the *Adams v. Richardson* (1972) litigation.[5] OCR's mission is "to ensure equal access to education and to promote educational excellence throughout the nation through vigorous enforcement of civil rights" (ED/Office for Civil Rights, 2000). One of the organization's primary responsibilities is to resolve discrimination complaints through enforcing one of five federal statutes.[6] This analysis concentrates on OCR's enforcement of just one of those statutes, Title VI of the Civil Rights Act of 1964. As noted earlier, Title VI prohibits discrimination in programs and activities that receive federal financial assistance. In the university environment, these programs and activities include, but are not limited to, admissions, recruitment, and financial aid.

In addition to OCR's enforcement of the nondiscrimination provisions of Title VI, it is involved in an oversight role of states' efforts to desegregate their public colleges and universities. This desegregation saga began approximately 30 years ago with the advent of the *Adams v. Richardson* (1972) litigation. Plaintiffs in *Adams v. Richardson* and its related cases relied on the enforcement of Title VI as their main argument to eliminate the dual system of higher education that had been established in 19 states. The 1890 Morrill Act "prohibited payments of federal funds to states that discriminated against blacks in admission to tax-supported colleges or who refused to provide 'separate but equal' facilities." Therefore, in accordance with the latter half of this clause, the following 19 states established dual public land-grant institutions: Alabama, Arkansas, Delaware, Florida, Georgia, Kentucky, Louisiana, Maryland, Mississippi, Missouri, North Carolina, Ohio, Oklahoma, Pennsylvania, South Carolina, Tennessee, Texas, Virginia, and West Virginia (Brown, 1999). The 1972 *Adams v. Richardson* decision ordered a remedy for Title VI violations through OCR; that is, OCR was to oversee the states' desegregation plans. That decision, however, did not mark the end of the controversy; it continued until 1990, when the *Adams v. Richardson* litigation died as a result of a court decision bearing the name of an intervenor in the case. *Women's Equity Action League* (1990) held that plaintiffs lacked a private right of action against a federal agency; consequently, the *Adams v. Richardson* litigation was dismissed (Brown, 1999). In 1992, individual states, not the federal government, were deemed to be the enforcers of Title VI desegregation compliance plans (Brown, 1999). *U.S. v. Fordice* (1992) held that it is the affirmative duty of the states to disestablish dual systems of higher education.

Policy Guidance
Public policy also must be considered in the present analysis. In 1994, the Department of Education issued policy guidelines that described Title VI's applicability to the distribution of race-based student financial aid (Department of Education, 1994). Five principles for awarding race-based funding are listed in this document, and the legal basis for each is given. The five principles are:

- Financial Aid for Disadvantaged Students;
- Financial Aid Authorized by Congress;
- Financial Aid to Remedy Past Discrimination;
- Financial Aid to Create Diversity; and,

Private Gifts Restricted by Race or National Origin (Department of Education, 1994).

This document provides solid guidance to universities; however, a university's adherence to the stated guidelines does not necessarily insulate it from suit.

Elimination of Certain Fellowship Programs

In addition to colleges and universities, federal agencies also have curtailed or eliminated their minority scholarship or fellowship programs. For example, effective 1999, the National Science Foundation (NSF) eliminated its Minority Graduate Research Fellowship program. This program had sponsored about 150 fellowships each year.[7] Legal controversy regarding this program arose in 1997, when Travis Kidd, a white graduate student from Clemson, sued the NSF (Cordes, Jan. 9, 1998). He alleged that the minority fellowship program, for which he applied and was rejected, illegally discriminated based on race because it was restricted to African Americans, Hispanic Americans, and Native Americans, and therefore constituted a quota system.

This lawsuit did not go to trial; rather, on the advice of the Department of Justice, it was settled about six months later (Cordes, July 3, 1998). Although NSF ended the program effective 1999, officials said that they planned to discontinue it in its challenged form before the settlement was reached. In 1998, NSF announced that it would sponsor a single Graduate Research Fellowship competition in which there would be "a single set of eligibility criteria, a unified review of applications, and a single set of fellowship awards" (S.W. Duby, personal communication, 1998).

The Patricia Roberts Harris Fellowship Program, a federal program for female and minority graduate students, was recently discontinued as well, effective during the 1999-2000 academic year. The Harris program was one of three graduate fellowships that the Department of Education provided for graduate students (Burd, 1998). The other two are the Jacob K. Javits Fellowship Program and the Graduate Assistance in Areas of National Need Program (GAANN), both of which continue to be offered.

The restructuring that has occurred as a result of these court decisions and federal programs reveal that admissions and financial aid programs that consider race are increasingly falling into disfavor. Upcoming decisions in the Michigan cases may further illustrate this trend.

The University of Texas

How have these legal decisions, adverse to affirmative action, affected recruitment practices, admissions and scholarship criteria, and enrollment patterns? It is interesting to consider the case of the University of Texas at Austin (UT– Austin). Since the *Hopwood* decision, Texas has been forbidden from considering race or ethnicity in its admissions and scholarship processes (Cooper, 2000). As discussed earlier, public institutions in Louisiana, Mississippi, and Texas, the other Fifth Circuit states, also are forbidden from considering race or ethnicity in the admissions process.

Enrollment Levels
As a result of the ban on considering applicants' races, UT-Austin's graduate and undergraduate minority enrollments suffered an overall decline. This declining enrollment has yet to rebound to pre-*Hopwood v. State of Texas* (1996) levels, with the exception of incoming first-year undergraduate minority enroll-ments, which have reached almost the same percentages as in 1996 (Carnevale, 1999; Cooper, 2000). First-year undergraduate African-American enrollment was 4.1% in Fall 1996, and 4.1% in Fall 1999; first-year undergraduate Hispanic enrollment was 14.5% in Fall 1996, and 13.9% in Fall 1999 (The University of Texas at Austin, 1999).

Minority Recruiting Practices – Undergraduate Level
It is interesting to note the actions taken by UT – Austin with respect to offering minority scholarships in light of the *Hopwood v. State of Texas* (1996) decision. In addition to being unable to consider race or ethnicity in the admissions process, the University of Texas was prohibited from awarding minority scholarships, as established in 1997 by the Texas' Attorney General, who broadened the Fifth Circuit's decision (Selingo, 1999; P. Reyes, personal communication, April 17, 2000). His successor rescinded this ruling, but told institutions of higher education not to use racial preferences. At the undergraduate level, however, minority students have been eligible to receive

certain types of funding without being specifically named. In 1999, a scholarship was created for students from high schools in low-income areas (Carnevale, 1999). Plus, UT's alumni association, not subject to the court decision, has offered scholarships to minority students (Carnevale, 1999). For example, in September 1999, The Ex-Students Association of UT-Austin distributed $800,000 to 200 minority students "to help fill in the gaps in financial aid" (Selingo, 1999). This Association has raised $4.2 million since *Hopwood v. State of Texas* (1996) for minority scholarships.

Also, UT-Austin uses an eight-factor "adversity index," established as a response to the *Hopwood v. State of Texas* (1996) decision, as a guide for offering admission and making scholarship awards to new students. The index factors in personal difficulties or challenges (Selingo, 1999). This "adversity index" is used as the basis for awarding two incoming undergraduate scholarships at UT-Austin: the "President's Achievement Scholarship" and the "Longhorn Opportunity Scholarship" (J. Wilcox, personal communication, April 18, 2000).

Award criteria for both scholarships rests mainly with the calculated "adversity index," with the second scholarship restricted to members of certain high schools. Eligible high schools are generally those in which the percentage of students sending their scores to UT is lower than the average. The average percentage per high school is 34%; that is, 34% of Texas high school students send their SAT scores to UT (J. Wilcox, personal communication, April 18, 2000).

The "adversity index" was designed in the following manner. University of Texas officials statistically analyzed the student population that they hoped to continue to recruit, and found that 90% shared similar characteristics. Some of these characteristics were incorporated into the "adversity index" (J. Wilcox, personal communication, April 18, 2000).

In using the "adversity index," values are determined for each of eight data elements (four of them are based on SAT data), inserted into a formula, and then a final number results. The eight data elements, specific to the student and the high school that the student attended, are:

- parental educational attainment;
- household income;

- percentage of high school enrollment categorized as economically disadvantaged;
- percentage of students in high school passing TAAS (Texas Achievement and Academic Skills, a mandatory test upon which the student must show a certain level of proficiency in order to graduate from high school);
- percentage of SAT-takers at the high school;
- percentage of students scoring higher on the SAT than Texas's suggested guideline for college-bound students;
- average SAT scores of students in high school; and,
- peer performance index, used to calculate student performance on the SAT relative to high school peers, calculated by the following formula: (student's SAT score/average SAT score of students in high school)/percentage of students scoring higher on the SAT than Texas's suggested guideline for college-bound students (J. Wilcox, personal communication, April 18, 2000).

The final number yielded from these eight data elements, known as the "Adversity Index Rating," is charted in a matrix: on an x-axis in four categories (limited, moderate, substantial, or extreme adversity) against the student's high school class rank on the y-axis. Matrix levels at which students are accepted do not operate as static "cut-offs;" they fluctuate from year to year depending on scores and funding levels (J. Wilcox, personal communication, April 18, 2000). Despite these fluctuations, generalizations can be made. For example, if a student is in the top 10% of her high school class and has experienced only "limited" adversity, she probably will not receive a "President's Achievement Scholarship."

Another non-race-based measure in undergraduate recruiting in Texas is the "10% plan." Under this plan, the top 10% of high school seniors at each high school are automatically admitted to Texas public colleges (Carnevale, 1999).[8] This policy, along with the recruiting efforts described above, applies only to the undergraduate level.

Texas is one of the 19 states that had a dual system of higher education that it must disestablish, yet four years ago with the *Hopwood v. State of Texas* (1996) decision, it became barred from considering race in the admissions process. Caught between a legal rock and a hard place, the state has found some interesting ways to operate within these legal boundaries. Other public institutions are located in states that must desegregate, but unlike the state of Texas, have not experienced a similar court ruling. These other institutions, however, are very aware that they could be sued at any time and currently are taking steps to avoid suit.

Conclusion

Over the last three decades, the legal, political, and social debate surrounding the concepts of nondiscrimination and affirmative action has reached a fever pitch in the realm of higher education admissions and student scholarships and fellowships. Once upholding the "educational benefit of diversity" justification for affirmative action admissions programs (*Regents v. Bakke,* 1978), courts have become more and more adverse, tending to strike such programs down, thereby shifting the standards under which these programs have been upheld in the past (*Podberesky v. Kirwan,* 1994/1995; *Hopwood v. State of Texas,* 1996). Decisions on pending litigation may provide clear direction, but final resolution of these cases is perhaps years away. Once Circuit Court decisions have been issued, however, there is no guarantee that the Supreme Court will hear an appeal of any of the cases. Although many expect the Court to grant *certiorari*, it may choose to deny this writ, in which case firm nationwide guidance would not be provided.

Public higher education in the United States is left to steer the best course it can among court decisions, federal nondiscrimination provisions, government oversight of desegregation, and public opinion to fashion the best environment possible for its entire university community. The answer to the question of whether adversity will replace diversity on a national scale, is, for now, elusive.

NOTES

1. The Fourth Circuit is comprised of Maryland, North Carolina, South Carolina, Virginia, and West Virginia.
2. The court described the underlying discrimination at UMCP as societal discrimination, as opposed to discrimination at the specific institution in question; as mentioned in the earlier discussion of *Regents v. Bakke* (1978), general societal discrimi-

nation cannot be used as a basis for supporting race-conscious remedies.

3. Initiative 200, passed in 1998, is an anti-affirmative action measure similar to California's Proposition 209, which was passed in 1996.

4. At that time as the Department of Health, Education, and Welfare.

5. This litigation will not be explained in depth because that is not the focus of this analysis, but will be discussed briefly.

6. The five federal statutes OCR is responsible for enforcing are: Title VI of the Civil Rights Act of 1964; Title IX of the Education Amendments of 1972; Section 504 of the Rehabilitation Act of 1973; the Age Discrimination Act of 1975; and, Title II of the Americans with Disabilities Act of 1990.

7. NSF also conducted a separate Graduate Research Fellowship program, which sponsored about 850 fellowships each year.

8. Similar measures are in place in California (4%) and in Florida (20%).

References

Barry, T. (1992). *Minority scholarships: Affirmative action or reverse discrimination?* ASPIRA Issue Brief.

Bowen, W.G. and Bok, D. (1998). *The shape of the river: Long-term consequences of considering race in college and university admissions.* Princeton, NJ: Princeton University Press.

Brown, II, M.C. (1999). *The quest to define collegiate desegregation: Black colleges, Title VI compliance, and Post-Adams litigation.* Westport, CT: Bergin & Garvey.

Burd, S. (compiled by). (1998). The Higher Education Amendments of 1998: The impact on colleges and students. *The Chronicle of Higher Education,* Oct. 16, 1998, p. A39.

Carnevale, D. (1999). Enrollment of minority freshmen nears pre-Hopwood levels at U. of Texas at Austin. *The Chronicle of Higher Education,* Sept. 3, 1999, p. A71.

Center for Individual Rights Home Page. (1997, March 6). University of Washington sued for discrimination [On-line]. Available: http://www.cir-usa.org/press_releases/smith_v_washington_pr.html

Clague, M.W. (1996). The missed link: Faculty "remnants" of Jim Crow and minority fellowship support programs. Institution for Higher Education Law and Governance, University of Houston, monograph 95-1. Paper presented November 1995 at the Annual Meeting of the Association for the Study of Higher Education, Orlando, Florida.

Cooper, K.J. (2000). Colleges testing new diversity initiatives: Success is uneven without traditional affirmative action. *The Washington Post*, April 2, 2000, p. A4.

Cordes, C. (1998). Lawsuit challenges science foundation's minority-fellowship program. *The Chronicle of Higher Education*, Jan. 9, 1998, p. A50.

Cordes, C. (1998). NSF agrees to settle white student's reverse-bias lawsuit. *The Chronicle of Higher Education*, July 3, 1998, p. A24.

ED/Office for Civil Rights: About Us! (2000). Available: http://www.ed.gov/offices/OCR/aboutus.html

Fact Sheet – University of Michigan. (2000). Available: http://www.umich.edu/~urel/admissions/faqs/facts.html

Foster, H. and Schubert, R. (1998). Two UW Law School applicants, two paths. *Seattle Post-Intelligencer*, October 15, 1998.

Hebel, S. (2000). U.S. appeals court upholds use of affirmative action in admissions. *The Chronicle of Higher Education*, Dec. 15, 2000, p. A40.

Hendrickson, R.M. (1996). The bell curve, affirmative action, and the quest for equity. In J. Kincheloe, S. Steinberg, and A. Gresson II (eds.), *Measured lies: The bell curve examined*. New York: St. Martin's Press.

Information on Admissions Lawsuits – University of Michigan. (2000) Available: http://www.umich. edu/~urel/admissions/faqs/lawqa.html

Law School admissions suit trial delayed. (2000). The University Record, April 10, 2000, Available: http://www.umich. edu/~urecord/9900/Apr10_00/12.htm

Numbers Bind. (1998). Review & Outlook (Editorial) *Wall Street Journal*, Sept. 3, 1998.

Selingo, J. (2000). U. of Massachusetts to limit use of race in admissions. *The Chronicle of Higher Education*, Jan. 21, 2000.

Selingo, J. (1999). Texas colleges seek new ways to attract minority students. *The Chronicle of Higher Education*, Nov. 19, 1999.

Selingo, J. (1999). Why minority recruiting is alive and well in Texas. *The Chronicle of Higher Education*, Nov. 19, 1999, p. A34.

The University of Texas at Austin, Office of Institutional Studies, Fall Enrollment by Level and Ethnicity: Percent Distribution. Available: http://www.utexas.edu/academic/ois/ stathb.99-00/s4b.html

Table of Legal Cases

Adams v. Richardson, 351 F.2d 636 (D.C. Cir. 1972).

Civil Rights Act of 1964, Pub. L. No. 88-352, 78 Stat. 241. Code of Federal Regulations.

Department of Education, Nondiscrimination in Federally Assisted Programs; *Title VI of the Civil Rights Act of 1964*; Notice. 59 Fed. Reg. 8756, Feb. 23, 1994.

Fourteenth Amendment, United States Constitution.

Gratz v. Bollinger, et al. No. 97-75231 (E.D. Mich. filed Oct. 14, 1997).

Grutter v. Bollinger, et al. No. 97-75928 (E.D. Mich. filed Dec. 3, 1997).

Grutter v. Bollinger, et al. and *Gratz v. Bollinger, et al.* (cases combined in resolving intervention issue) 188 F.3d 394 (6th Cir. 1999).

Hopwood v. State of Texas, 78 F.3d 932 (5th Cir. 1996), *cert. denied*, 518 U.S. 1033 (1996).

Hopwood v. State of Texas, 999 F.Supp. 872 (W.D. Tex. 1998).

Maryland Troopers Association v. Evans, 993 F.2d 1072, 1076 (4th Cir. 1993).

Podberesky v. Kirwan, 38 F.3d 147 (4th Cir. 1994), *cert. denied*, 514 U.S. 1128 (1995).

Regents of the University of California v. Bakke, 438 U.S. 265 (1978).

Second Morrill Act (1890).

Smith v. University of Washington Law School, Civ. No. C97-335Z (W.D. Wash. 1999).

U.S. v. Fordice, 505 U.S. 717 (1992).

Women's Equity Action League v. Cavazos, 906 F.2d 742 (D.C. Cir. 1990).

CHAPTER 8

THE TRAGEDY OF REJECTING A VIABLE SOLUTION FOR THE DEVELOPMENT OF SUCCESSFUL COLLEGIATE ACADEMIC INCENTIVE PROGRAMS FOR AFRICAN AMERICANS

William T. Trent & Timothy K. Eatman

*The question in this case is whether a public university, racially segregated by law for almost a century and actively resistant to integration for at least twenty years thereafter, may – after confronting the injustices of its past – voluntarily seek to remedy the resulting problems of its present, by spending **one percent** of its financial aid budget to provide scholarships to approximately thirty high-achieving African-American students each year.[1]*

J. Frederick Motz (emphasis added)

Introduction

United States District Judge J. Frederick Motz offers a concise and insightful summary of the *Podberesky v. Kirwan* litigation in the above excerpt taken from the opening of his opinion, which responded to the remand ordered by the Court of Appeals for the Fourth Circuit. This quote points to the prevailing question of the case: how can an institution, within the parameters of the law, make up for a history of discrimination against a group of people? It also serves as a reminder of the persisting difficulty of race relations in American society. The court of appeals ruling raises anew the question of what constitutes manifest vestiges of past discrimination.

On appeal by the plaintiff, Daniel J. Podberesky, the court overturned the initial ruling. According to their interpretation of law, Judge Motz had improperly ruled in favor of the defendant, The University of Maryland at College Park (hereafter referred to as UMCP or the University), because he did not find *justifiable* present effects of past discrimination (*Podberesky V. Kirwan*, 1992). This follows from a focal point of the defense case, which posited the notion that the poor reputation of UMCP in the surrounding "minority" community was sufficient to establish the continued presence of discrimination. Without adding any further clarification to the initial ruling, the United States Supreme Court implicitly endorsed the ruling of the Fourth Circuit by refusing to hear the case. The obvious message this refusal conveys is that the Supreme Court also believes that the reputation of the University in the "minority" community is not a permissible argument to establish vestiges of past discrimination (Winston, 1995).

That the reputation and legacy of the University of Maryland in the minds of the local citizenry is reasonably linked to present harms is arguable. Many agree that the worth of a viable institution is determined in part by its reputation. Indeed, several expert witnesses in the case have noted this important dynamic as a powerful indicator of the status of UMCP in the community.[2] However, at best, it is only one of the manifest vestiges of discrimination. At least equally compelling is the persistence of disparities between students of color and whites in enrollment, achievement, attrition, and quality of educational experience.

The Benjamin Banneker Scholars program (hereafter referred to as Banneker or BBSP) is an example of one program that evolved out of the 1970s as a way of redressing educational inequity. Many similar efforts have been established at U.S colleges and universities, each requiring consideration and sensitivity to the current racial politics and to other social dynamics on the campuses. The University of Michigan Rackham Scholars Program is another example of this type of intervention effort[3]. The success and efficient handling of the BBSP is only amplified by the minimal investment of UMCP resources required for its operation, and the existence of several other Banneker type programs at other universities around the country which are experiencing success in the effort to address honestly the historical violations of individual rights in higher education and the current need for access and success on the part of African Americans.

The goal of this chapter is to underscore what is a very important, yet overlooked facet, of interpreting *Podberesky*. The understanding that, despite the desperate need, a program, which was experiencing substantial and measurable successes in creatively addressing a major educational challenge has been recast. We argue that virtually dismissed in the wake of the appeals court decision is the extent to which the Benjamin Banneker Scholars Program was effective.

The underlying critique of this work points to what we think is the unfortunate trend in society to underestimate the foundation of American racism. The court of appeals ruling in *Podberesky* is an important example of the manifestation of this trend in the realm of jurisprudence as related to the context of higher education. The philosophical basis for this trend is the idea that America is now a society where color is no longer an issue – a society that has met the challenges so aptly identified by W.E.B. Dubois as the challenge of the twentieth century; the problem of the color line (Dubois, 1953).

Historical Context

The University of Maryland should be commended for developing the Benjamin Banneker Scholars program in an era when many institutions and noted commentators were more concerned with explaining away disparities rather than finding solutions for them. These critics usually blame victims of discrimination for the disparities, ignore the historical context of the disparities, and some have even gone as far as denying the continued existence of racism on college campuses (Bloom, 1987; D'Souza, 1991; McWhorter, 2000; National Academy of Scholars, 2000; Schlesinger, 1991). The integrity of UMCP's ameliorative efforts is especially notable given the history of higher education in Maryland.

UMCP became Maryland's land-grant institution under the 1862 Morrill Land Grant Act (Morrill Land Grant Act-I, 1862), and, until 1916, only White males could attend the university. At that time, White women were permitted entry. Although four institutions for the education of African Americans were established between 1866 and 1909 and chartered by the state, none received substantial state aid despite the provisions of *Morrill II* (Morrill Land Grant Act-II, 1890).

As was typical of most institutions that would admit Blacks at this time, these four were not accredited and conducted programs considered far inferior to the rigor of programs and state supported institutions for Whites.

Evidence of the *de jure* segregation that was prevalent in the state at this time is found in arrangements Maryland made to pay out of state tuition rather than integrate its own colleges; these practices lasted until the 1950s. There were few cases where Blacks successfully sued for admission to Maryland institutions. Probably most notable is the order won by Thurgood Marshall directing that Donald Murray be admitted to the University of Maryland Law School (*Pearson v. Murray*, 1936). Despite the sense of hope that this created, this victory did not translate into a watershed of equity.

It was not until after the *Brown* decision (*Brown v. Board of Education*, 1954) that university officials slowly began to remove the enrollment prohibition imposed upon Blacks. Twenty years later the threat of losing federal funding provided by the *Adams* (*Adams v. Richardson*, 1973) litigation became the impetus for UMCP to grant equity concessions articulated in the form of a five-year desegregation plan. This plan relied heavily on the use of "other-race" financial aid as a desegregation tool. The Banneker program, established in 1978 is a direct outgrowth from that desegregation plan. We maintain that the critical importance of historical context cannot be overstated when considering issues and strategies of redress.

The Concept of Special Academic Programs for "Minorities" and Program Components

The enactment of social legislation during the Kennedy and Johnson Administrations provided an impetus for the development of greater educational opportunity for America's youth at all levels of our society. With the passage of the Economic Opportunity Act of 1964 and subsequent titles, educational researchers developed a greater interest in the effect that institutions of higher education had upon youth from disadvantaged and poor backgrounds who were being enrolled in special academic programs. Since this time, the federal government has supported programs for the disadvantaged starting with preschool (Headstart) through higher education. Traditionally, funding was conducted largely through the Office of Economic Opportunity, the United States Office of Education, and various offices within the Department of Health Education and Welfare.

It should be noted that Congress approved the National Direct Student Loan Program in 1959. The Elementary and Secondary Education Act and the Higher Education Act – both enacted in 1955 – are evidence of the role of federal support to various educational programs. Specifically, the Higher Education Act provided numerous opportunities: aid to small colleges and developing institutions through cooperative programs and national teaching fellowships; aid to exchange faculty members, exchange students, visiting scholars; the sharing of libraries and laboratories; financial assistance for community service and continuing education programs; federal scholarships, student loan programs, and work-study opportunities.[4]

The contributions of private foundations are also noteworthy since Ford, Rockefeller, Carnegie, Sloan, and others made initial grants to universities and colleges, school districts, and educational organizations to deal with the educational problems of poor and disadvantaged youth in urban depressed areas. Much of the emphasis was concentrated in large metropolitan cities, which were experiencing, for the first time, the effect of schooling upon their "minority" populations. In fact one of the most influential grants made to programs for the disadvantaged was the Ford Foundation's Great Cities Project – a grant to large cities for the purpose of developing a "massive and integrated attack upon the problems of education in urban depressed areas" (Gordon & Wilkerson, 1966).

Because of the history of past discrimination and the evidence of present effects, typically these programs have required significantly greater effort than programs for the traditional student. Broad support for these programs has been celebrated where the concept has been framed as promoting equity. However, as some conservative media specialists have begun to suggest the notion of "preferential" treatment due to race in the context of these programs, there has been a backlash where their legal and moral basis has been challenged.

The Benjamin Banneker Scholars Program

The state of Maryland was one of nineteen southern and border states cited in *Adams v. Richardson* (1973) as having operated a dual system of higher education, one for African Americans and one for Whites, and ordered to devise specific plans for dismantling that structure. UMCP, the flagship of the state system, was to undertake specific steps to desegregate its student body. Among the steps taken was the implementation of the Benjamin Banneker Scholars Program, originating in 1978 and beginning its first year of operation in 1979-1980.

This was, however, by no means a simple, timely, or agreeable endeavor. UMCP, even after establishing the Committee on Meaningful Integration in the mid-sixties, did little to advance the desegregation mandate. It is no wonder that the UMCP experienced the rejection of four compliance plans by the U.S. Office of Civil Rights. Each time it was an action on the part of UMCP policy that either directly or indirectly contradicted the affirmations set forth in the desegregation plan. It was not until June 3, 1985, that OCR accepted the "1985-89" plan as being in compliance with Title VI of the 1964 Civil Rights Act.

As part of this plan, The Benjamin Banneker Scholars (BBSP) program, which had been established almost ten years earlier, assumed a different role from when it was initially established. It was enhanced as one of UMCP's most important recruitment efforts. BBSP targeted academically talented "minority" students and provided scholarship aid regardless of financial need. The size of the scholarship assistance, the range of services provided "scholars" and the racial designation of the targeted "minority" students has each evolved. The consistent feature has been a focus on increasing the representation of African Americans on the College Park campus, especially as it furthered the implementation of the State's Desegregation Plan and the commitment to the recruitment and retention of African American students.

Data

Descriptive and inferential statistics are used to illustrate the significant success of BBSP. The analyses presented below are based on data provided by UMCP in its efforts to respond to litigation in *Podberesky v. Kirwan* challenging the constitutionality of the Banneker Scholars Program because it is reserved exclusively for high achieving African American students.

There are three data sources used to compile the results presented below. These are: UMCP registration data for the years 1974 through 1990; UMCP application data for the years 1974 through 1990; and, UMCP financial aid data covering the years 1974 through 1990. In addition, annual reports on the *Plan to Assure Equal Postsecondary Educational Opportunity 1985-89* (Maryland Higher Education Commission, May 1991); *Final Update Of The Plan To Assure Equal Postsecondary Educational Opportunity At The University of Maryland At College Park* (May 1990); and, *Institutional Studies – Progress Reports University of Maryland at College Park* (1981 through 1991) were provided by the Maryland Attorney General's Office. These reports provide summary counts on enrollment, retention, degree attainment, applications and acceptances by race, ethnicity and sex for the College Park campus and the public postsecondary colleges and universities.

The results presented below examine several specific questions designed to explore the impact of the Banneker aid program on its recipients. The broad question explored herein is "Does the Benjamin Banneker Scholars Program aid in the recruitment and retention of African American students?"

More specifically, these analyses focus on:

- retention, comparing the graduation rates of Banneker recipients with recipients of other forms of aid and students with no aid for entering cohorts beginning in 1979;
- retention, comparing the graduation rates of students by race and SAT verbal and SAT math quartiles for entering cohorts beginning in 1974;
- performance, comparing the average cumulative GPA, for each of five years, of Banneker recipients with those for recipients of other forms of aid or no aid, by entering cohort beginning in 1974;
- performance, comparing the average cumulative GPA, for each of five years, for all students by race, and high school GPA for entering cohorts beginning in 1974;
- performance, comparing the major field concentrations of Banneker degree recipients with the major field degree

concentrations of recipients of other forms of aid or no aid by cohort, beginning in 1974;
- persistence, comparing the graduation rates of Banneker recipients with recipients of other forms of aid and those who received no aid, across categories of high school grade point average, SAT verbal and SAT math quartiles for each cohort;
- recruitment, monitoring the apparent trend in African American students in the highest SAT quartiles from 1974 through 1991.

Description of the Data
The first three data sources named above, registration data, applications data, and financial aid data, used for a portion of these analyses are from the archival data system at the UMCP. These are historical files containing student level data from the university's information on student applicants, registrants, and financial aid recipients. The Office of Institutional Studies supplied two magnetic data files: Registration Summary Records and Applicant file. The Administrative Computer Center provided one magnetic tape: the Historic and Current Award file. From these three files an aggregated file was created, resulting in a file containing comprehensive data for 81,634 students based on the cohort year in which they entered. The eighty-one thousand plus records provide a nearly complete, very useful and clear set of data upon which the findings reported below are based. The variables and their frequencies are presented in figures one through six.

Figure 1. Frequency Distribution by Cohort Year.

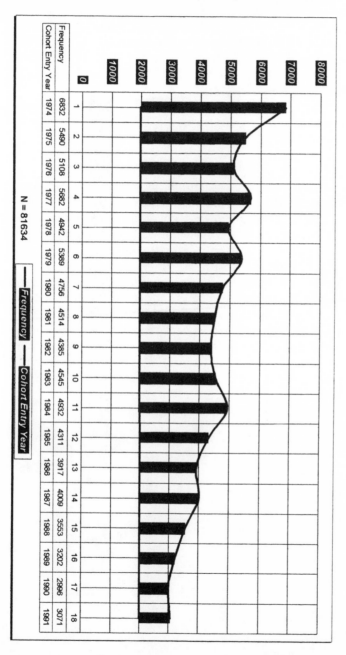

Figure 2. Frequency Distribution of Race constructed UMCP Student Database, 1974-1991.

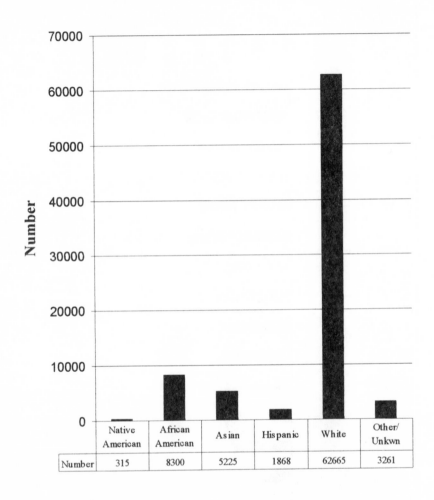

Number	Native American	African American	Asian	Hispanic	White	Other/ Unkwn
	315	8300	5225	1868	62665	3261

Figure 3. Financial Aid.

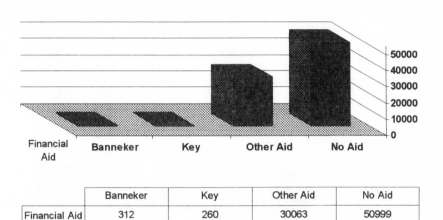

	Banneker	Key	Other Aid	No Aid
Financial Aid	312	260	30063	50999

Figure 4. High School Grade Point Average.

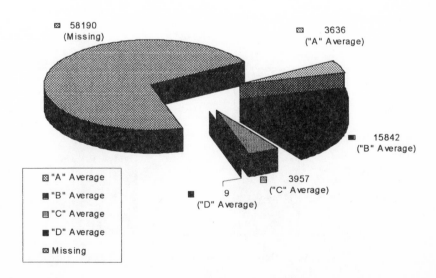

Figure 5. Years to Graduation.

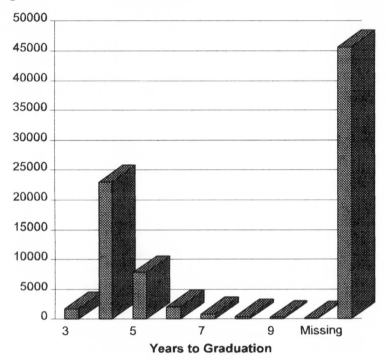

Figure 6. Degree Attained.

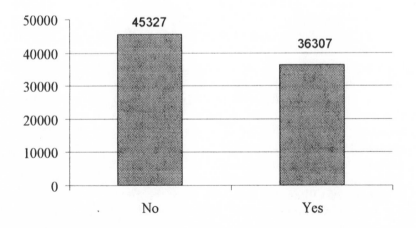

Analysis of the Constructed Data Findings

The results presented below rely on both a description of the data presented in table form and multivariate analyses to identify the strength of relationship between being a Banneker recipient and selected outcomes – graduation and final grade point average. The findings from the constructed U. Md. data can be quickly summarized. These analyses show that:

- Being a recipient of a Benjamin Banneker Scholar award is beneficial for persistence, retention, performance, and graduation;
- There is evidence that the implementation of BBSP resulted in a meaningful and sustained increase in the number of academically talented African American students who entered the University of Maryland-College Park.
- The strength of the statistical significance of the relationship between being a Banneker recipient and graduating or earning a higher grade point average is substantial and confirms the patterns shown in the descriptive tables.

Given the consistency of these findings in these data, it can be argued that the Banneker Scholars program substantially meets its intended purposes.

Retention
These analyses explore retention first by examining graduation rates by cohort, aid type, and race. African American students graduated at a rate ranging from a low of 26.9% for the cohort entering in 1978 to a high of 39% for the cohort entering in 1986. The 1987 cohort shows a rate of 25%, but is not considered here because the Maryland data only covers through 1991 and a substantial number of students take five years to graduate.

Recipients of the Banneker Scholars award graduate at a rate that exceeds the graduation rates of African American students receiving other forms of aid or no aid. Beginning in 1979, the first recorded year for a Banneker Scholars award, two of the three African American recipients of the award are reported as having graduated (66.7%) compared to 67.5% of 120 African American recipients of Other Aid and 24% of 316 African Americans who are reported receiving No Aid. By 1981 African American recipients of the Banneker Scholars award are reported graduating at a rate of 86.7%. For the years 1982 through 1987, the reported graduation rates for African American recipients of the Banneker Scholar award are 80%(n=15), 90.5%(n=21), 75% (n=16), 83.3%(n=24), 65.4%(n=26), and 77.8%(n=18).

Overall, Banneker recipients in each SAT quartile graduate at a higher rate than is apparent for students in that same quartile when aid is not considered. For example, Banneker recipients in the 1983 cohort, third SAT verbal quartile graduated at the rate of 81.8%. By contrast, overall, African Americans in the 1983 cohort, third quartile show a graduation rate of 54.3%. It must be acknowledged that the numbers of African American Banneker recipients is small relative to the total pool of African American students. Nevertheless, the difference in graduation rates favors Banneker recipients even when contrasted with other aid recipients in the same cohort.

Performance

A third approach to assessing the impact of Banneker on retention is an examination of the cumulative GPA by cohort, aid type, and race for each of five consecutive years. The results here clearly favor African American students who are Banneker recipients. For the 1980 cohort, the mean cumulative GPA for African American Banneker recipients was higher than that of any other African American students for all years. In general, African American Banneker recipients show a higher cumulative grade point average for each year for all cohorts compared to other African American students and is also higher than all other students except students who received the Key Scholarship.

Adding high school GPA into the analysis adds another dimension to the findings. African American students who were "A" or "B" students in high school seldom sustain mean cumulative GPAs that rival those of Banneker recipients in the same cohort. This analysis suggests two interpretations: that the process used to select Banneker Scholars effectively identifies very capable students; that experiences associated with being a Banneker Scholar facilitate higher achievement, or some combination of the two.

A different assessment of performance is presented when we examine the major fields in which students are concentrated. A desirable outcome would be that Banneker recipients would show a greater concentration of their degrees in those major fields – science and technical majors – that are traditionally less accessible to African American students. Such a result would suggest that African American students who are Banneker recipients are contributing to a greater likelihood of an increased African American presence in related areas as professionals.

The distributions of the major field concentrations by broad Major Field by Aid Type, and Race for each Cohort. These results show that among African American students, those with no aid have fared well in the science and technical fields, showing just over a quarter to more than a third of their concentration in these fields from 1974 through 1979. This suggests the speculation that African American students with no aid were from socioeconomic and academic backgrounds that sustained their academic pursuits. Beginning in 1980 and continuing through 1991, Banneker recipients performed as well or better compared to other African American students who majored in a science or technical field. In sum, African American students who were Banneker recipients show as high a concentration in science and technical fields as their African American peers and generally exceeding the concentration shown for Whites in these fields. Only students who were recipients of the Key Scholarship show consistently higher concentrations in science and technical fields. African American students in increasing numbers also sought degrees in Business/Economics during the 1980s and African American Banneker recipients were well represented in these fields.

African American Banneker recipients in each cohort graduate at a higher rate in all fields compared to other African American students. Generally, their rate of graduation in any field is second only to recipients of the Key Scholarship and that is mainly limited to graduation rates in the science and technical category.

In summary, with respect to these descriptive assessments of performance, each indicates that the Banneker Scholar's award makes a substantial difference to recipients. In general:

- each cohort shows a higher Grade Point Average for each consecutive year of enrollment up to and including their 5th year compared to other African American students.
- each cohort shows a higher graduation rate for Banneker recipients even among students with comparable high

school grade point averages among African American students.
- each cohort shows African American Banneker recipients with higher concentrations in Science and Technical Major Fields that have traditionally been less accessible to African American students.
- each cohort shows African American Banneker recipients with higher graduation rates in Science and Technical Major Fields that have traditionally been less accessible to African American students.

Most impressive in these results are those findings that show these performance indicators for African American recipients of the Banneker Scholars award to come closest to those of their White counterparts at the University of Maryland, College Park.

Recruitment
Analysis of graduation rates by SAT verbal and math quartile, respectively, by race for each cohort provide an indirect assessment of the impact of the Banneker program on the recruitment of African American students. The examination of the number of African American students in the highest SAT quartiles beginning in 1974, five years prior to the implementation of BBSP and any increments in this category following the implementation of the program, reflect an important characteristic of students at the point of enrollment. From 1974 through 1979, the number of African Americans graduating who initially fell in the highest SAT Verbal quartile, ranged from a low of 10 in 1975 to a high of 19 in 1974. The total never reached the 20s. Beginning in 1980, the number of African Americans in this category reached 38 and did not drop below that number until 1990 when it fell to 32. In effect, these data would suggest that the implementation of the Banneker program, either directly or indirectly, facilitated the enrollment and success of at least twice as many African American students in the high SAT verbal quartile.

Multivariate analyses were conducted to examine the strength of association between being a Banneker recipient and selected outcomes. The outcomes that are examined are graduation and cumulative grade point average. These analyses are conducted only for the African American recipients of the award. Two regression procedures are used in these analyses. To examine the graduation outcome, "graduated" vs. "did not graduate," a logistic regression is used because the dependent variable is dichotomous. The cumulative grade point measure is a continuous variable and a standard ordinary least squares regression procedure is used.

There are three tests of the relationship between Banneker recipients and graduation rates; each test asks "how well can we predict graduation using the included measures?" The first test uses the student's SAT verbal and math scores, high school grade point average, cohort and financial aid – defined as a three category variable – Banneker (Aid 1) and Other Aid (Aid 2) and No Aid (Aid =0). The second test omits the math SAT score because of the missing data for that measure. The third test eliminates all except the cohort and financial aid variables. The results reveal that each test correctly predicts more than 75% of the cases with respect to graduation or failure to graduate. The model containing just the cohort and financial aid variables correctly predicts 75.43% of the cases; the model containing all but the SAT Math variable correctly predicts 81.28% of the cases and, the model containing all measures correctly predicts the graduation status of 81.41% of the cases. In sum, using just the cohort and financial measures, the graduation status of three-fourths of the cases is correctly determined. Adding the additional measures only increases predictive ability by 6 percentage points. Most importantly, the strongest predictor in each model is the aid category that represents Banneker (Aid 1). Each model is significant at the probability level of .0000 and the Banneker aid category is significant at roughly the same level. These results reinforce the findings which show the graduation rates in descriptive form. Receiving a Banneker award is shown to be substantively and statistically significant as a determinant of graduation. Moreover, when compared with the coefficients for SAT scores and high school grade point average, it is a somewhat more important contributor to graduation.

Summary

These findings, derived from the constructed University of Maryland-College Park data provide substantial evidence of the significance of the Banneker Scholars program for African American students and, by extension, the University. BBSP is shown to increase persistence to graduation; sustain higher academic performance; contribute to the access and success of African American students in science and technical fields; and, appears to have contributed to increases in the number of higher achieving African American students enrolling in and completing the University of Maryland-College Park. Finally, these data also provide evidence that the program contributions are statistically significant for graduation and academic performance.

HEGIS/IPEDS Analysis

The HEGIS/IPEDS data on opening fall enrollment were used to show the racial composition of undergraduate enrollment trends for the state of Maryland and its public institutions, particularly the University of Maryland, College Park campus. The enrollment data are available for the fall semester of alternating years beginning in 1976 and ending with the fall of 1990. These data are used to examine the following questions:

- What is the trend in African American fulltime student enrollment in the public colleges and universities in the state of Maryland for the period covered by these data, in absolute terms and relative to other race and ethnic categories?
- What is the trend in African American fulltime student enrollment in the University of Maryland at College Park for the period covered by these data, in absolute terms and relative to other race and ethnic categories?

The HEGIS/IPEDS data on earned degrees and completions will be used to show the racial composition of degrees awarded at the undergraduate level for the state of Maryland and its public institutions, particularly the University of Maryland, College Park campus. The earned degree data are available for alternating academic years beginning in 1976 and ending with academic year 1990-91. These data will be used to examine the following questions:

- What is the trend in bachelors degrees earned by African American students from the public colleges and universities in the state of Maryland for the period covered by these data in absolute terms and relative to other race and ethnic categories?

- What is the trend in bachelors' degrees earned by African American students from the University of Maryland for the period covered by these data in absolute terms and relative to other race/ethnic categories?
- What are the trends in bachelors' degrees earned by African American students, by major field, from public colleges and universities in the state of Maryland for the period covered by these data, in absolute terms and relative to other race and ethnic categories?
- What are the trends in bachelors' degrees earned by African American students, by major field, from the University of Maryland at College Park for the period covered by these data, in absolute terms and relative to other race and ethnic categories?

The results discussed below cover the period 1976 through 1990 for enrollment and 1976-77 through 1989-90 for degree attainment. In those instances where data were not available from the HEGIS/IPEDS data, reports from the University of Maryland, Office of Institutional Studies were used to supplement the HEGIS/IPEDS data. This only occurred for the degree attainment data for the years 1982-83, 1984, and 1990-91.

Enrollment Trends
The trend summaries for the enrollment data for First-Time Full-Time Freshman Enrollments at University of Maryland at College Park by year and race follows that of national trends for African American students; 1976 is shown as a high point for first-time freshman enrollments followed by declines through 1982. For 1984 through 1990, there is a somewhat even pattern. In 1976 African American first-time full-time enrollment totaled 496 at the College Park campus and dropped to 405 in 1982. It reached 496 again in 1988 and in 1990 the total was 473.

These actual counts give a different view of trends from the corresponding percentages which change very little from 1976 through 1984. There is a low of 8.8% in 1978 and a high of 9.7% in 1982 but these are the two lowest years in terms of actual count, 423 and 405 respectively. Similarly, 1986, 1988 and 1990 show percentages that could be misinterpreted to mean that African American enrollment had increased dramatically, showing 12.1%, 13.7% and 15.3% respectively. What has occurred according to these data is a decrease in the total size of the first time full time enrollment of white students. Both in actual number and as a percentage of the total, White students show a dramatic decline from 1976 through 1990. They show an 85.3% share in 1976 (n=4,446) but only a 66.2% share in 1990 (n=2,040).

Trend analysis for full-time undergraduates presents a pattern somewhat different for African American students when examining actual counts. In this analysis, the decline is between the years 1980 and 1982, from 1,828 students to 1,743 students. From 1982 to 1990, there is a clear pattern of increase, from 1,743 students to 2,416 students. These are impressive numbers, indicating either high retention or longer time to graduation. This consistency of increase also corresponds to the time period during which the Banneker program improved its aid package and the number of students served. In this trend both the actual numbers and the percentages seem more appropriate. The percentage increase for African Americans is from 7.9% to 11.2% from 1976 to 1990. Nonetheless, there is a notable decline for white full time under-graduates, from 19,319 (85.9%) in 1976 to 15,448 (71.7%) in 1990.

One issue raised when colleges and universities seek to increase their minority enrollment is whether or not they do so by "loading up" on entering freshmen but not retaining them through later years. If the freshmen count is a high proportion of the undergraduate count we could argue that retention is low; however, analysis suggests just the opposite for African American students and Hispanic students, in particular, but also for all students. The ratio was higher for African American and Hispanic students in 1976 (27.8% and 27%, respectively) but reached parity with other groups in the succeeding years suggesting an improving retention rate. This ratio must be read cautiously however, given that the decreasing size of entering classes from 1984 to 1990 distorts this ratio during those years.

Upon analysis of all public colleges in Maryland, a different pattern of African American first-time full-time freshman enroll-ment for all public colleges emerges. First, 1976 shows the lowest enrollment of the eight time points (2,023) and 1990 the highest (3,246). Total African American first-time full-time enrollment in 1978 was the previous high (2,914) followed by a decline to 2,312 in 1986 and then an increase to 2,569 in 1988.

The pattern for African American full-time undergraduate enrollment for all public colleges mirrors that for the College Park campus. Full-time African American undergraduate enrollment was high in 1976 (12,086) and declined through 1984 (10,109). The increase occurs in 1986 (10,546) and the 1990 count (13,046) exceeds the 1976 count. White full-time undergraduate enrollments does not fluctuate for these schools as it did for the College Park campus. It actually increased from 1976 (n=38,633) to 1988 (46,224) and declined in 1990 (43,612). For 1976 to 1990, white full time undergraduate enrollment increased by a net change of 4,979 students, a 12.9% increase compared to the 7.9% increase for African Americans over the same period.

The examination of these enrollment trends shows a somewhat clear pattern both for first-time full-time freshmen and full time undergraduates at the College Park campus. We can conclude that the overall stability in incoming African American students is clear and that the students appear to be persisting based on the actual count of African American undergraduates and the ratio of freshmen to undergraduates.

Degree Attainment Trends

From 1976 to 1990, the total number of earned degrees awarded to African Americans at the College Park campus, increased substantially from 255 to 422, a 65% increase. The critical years in this increase appear to be 1986 and forward. It is important to note that this would be four years following the full funding of the Banneker Scholars program and hence the program could well contribute to these increases. The percentage increase during this period is less misleading than those for enrollment but are subject to the same concern in that they sometimes mask a smaller total.

The more convincing aspect of the success of efforts at the College Park campus can be found in examining the results of African American earned degree totals for all Maryland public colleges including UMCP and for the individual campuses. The net change for all public colleges from 1976 to 1988 – 1,691 (12.6%) to 1,928 (12.5%), or a gain of 227 – is a 13.4% increase compared to the 65% increase for UMCP. Indeed, the net change for the College Park Campus is more than twice as the net change for the rest of the system, since the increase at UMCP was 167 and the rest of the schools contribute only 60 graduates to the increase.

The final area addressed with these data is to explore degree concentrations. An important aspect of increased minority access to flagship universities is the opportunity to gain access to those science and technical fields that are unavailable or limited in other colleges. There is clear evidence of the importance of access when we contrast African American degree concentrations for 1976 and 1988 of UMCP. The first and most informative change is from 3 degrees in engineering in 1976 to 29 degrees in engineering in 1988. That is a change from 1% to 8% of their earned degrees. Small increases – from 2 to 5 for mathematics; from 9 to 11 in biology – occur in other science and technical fields. The next major increase occurred in Business where the number doubled from 30 in 1976 to 61 in 1988. These patterns show limited evidence that the African American students enrolling in and completing their work at the College Park campus are persisting better in the more challenging fields and competing well with their other-race counterparts.

The results from the examination of these degree data show a clear pattern of overall increase and a clear pattern of increased dispersion across major fields for African American students attending the University of Maryland at College Park. Notably, the onsets of the positive patterns correspond to the full implementation of the Banneker Scholars program. While the HEGIS/IPEDS data do not allow a direct assessment of BBSP, these results conform well to the patterns reported in the constructed data from the University of Maryland presented above.

Conclusion

Taken together, these two sets of analyses, from the different databases, provide substantial evidence of the value of the Banneker Scholars award program. It was found to influence retention, persistence, performance and graduation rates positively for African American students. It was also found to contribute to increased recruitment of high achieving students. That latter finding would appear to be borne out in two results. First, in the analysis of the UMCP data on graduation by SAT quartiles that showed that the numbers of African American students in the highest quartile enrolling at UMCP increased substantially following 1980, after the implementation of BBSP. Second, the HEGIS/IPEDS data show both an increase in earned degrees for African American students at UMCP and an increasing concentration of those degrees being earned in the more challenging science and technical fields, especially Engineering. This latter result certainly suggests that the African American students earning degrees in these fields might be more talented.

On the basis of these findings the program appears to fully meet its intended objectives of reducing segregation at the College Park campus, providing increase access to African American students and reducing segregation between departments on campus. If it is indeed accomplishing these objectives, it can not help but have the added benefit of enhancing the status of African American students on campus and improving race relations. In the opinion of the authors, it is a program that should receive increased support.

Notes

1. Opinion of the United States District Court for the District of Maryland.
2. See Allen, Blackwell, Feagin, Trent and the memorandum from Attorney General of MD.
3. See Rackham report.
4. Harcleroad (1970) and Passow (1968) have described the support of such programs by federal funds.

References

Bloom, A. (1987). *The closing of the American mind.* New York: Simon & Schuster.

D'Souza, D. (1991). *Illiberal education: The politics of race and sex on campus.* New York: Free Press.

Dubois, W. E. B. (1953). *The Souls of Black Folk* (1996 Modern Library Edition ed.). New York: Blue Heron.

Gordon, E. W. & Wilkerson, D. A. (1966). *Compensatory education for the disadvantaged.* New York: College Entrance Examination Board.

Harcleroad, F. (Ed). (1970). *Issue of the seventies.* San Francisco: Jossey-Bass.

McWhorter, J. H. (2000). *Losing the race: Self-sabotage in Black America.* New York: Free Press.

National Academy of Scholars (2000). *Brief of national Academy of Scholars as amicus curaie in support of plaintiffs' motion for partial summary judgment. B. M. Clagett, O.M. Garibaldi, and K.A. Noreika.* Washington, D. C.: Covington & Burling, Attorneys at Law.

Passow, H.A. (1968). *Developing programs for the educationally disadvantaged.* New York: Teachers College Press.

Schlesinger, A. M. (1991). *The disuniting of America: Reflections on a multicultural society.* Knoxville, Tenn: Whittle Direct Books.

Winston, J. A. (1995). *Letter to college and university counsel regarding the Podberesky case.* Washington, D.C.: United States Department of Education.

Table of Legal Cases

Adams v. Richardson, 480 F. 2d 1159 (1973).

Brown v. Board of Education, 347 U.S. 483 (1954).

Morrill Land Grant Act - I, 12 Stat.503,7 U.S.C.301 et.seq. (1862).

Morrill Land Grant Act - II, ch.841, 26 Stat.417, 7 U.S.C. 322 et seq.(1890).

Pearson V. Murray, 169 Md. 478, 182 A. 590 (1936).
Podberesky V. Kirwan, 956 F.2d 52-4th Cir. (1992).

CHAPTER 9

ACADEMIC ACCESS AND EQUAL OPPORTUNITY: RETHINKING THE FOUNDATIONS FOR POLICY ON DIVERSITY

Edward P. St. John & Glenda D. Musoba

For a very brief period in the 1970s, public policy was aligned with the goal of overcoming the vestiges of segregation in American higher education. After centuries of legal segregation, the federal courts began to promote desegregation of public colleges after the *Adams* decision in 1977 (Williams, 1988). This reform effort built on a strong foundation provided by the Great Society education reforms of President Johnson. Federal student aid programs were organized around the principle of promoting equal opportunity and were adequately funded (Gladieux & Wolanin, 1976), and school reform focused on improving opportunity for historically disadvantaged students (Wong, in press). In the late 1970s, traditional college-age African Americans participated in higher education at essentially the same rate as Whites (U.S. Department of Education, 1998). Unfortunately, soon after the 1980 election of Ronald Reagan the federal government essentially dismantled the entire structure of federal policies that promoted equal opportunity and diversity in higher education.

At the start of the twenty-first century, a new set of public policies no longer overtly supports improvements in diversity. During the middle 1990s, federal policy on higher education desegregation shifted from promoting desegregation of predominantly White colleges to promoting the desegregation of historically Black colleges (St. John & Hossler, 1998; Williams, 1997), before all of the *Adams* states had their initial plans approved by the federal government (Brown & Hendrickson, 1997; Williams, 1997). School reform shifted to a focus on outcomes – and to an overt emphasis on standardized tests – replacing the former emphasis on ensuring equal opportunity and equal resources (Finn, 1990). Federal student grants declined during the last two decades of the century, increasing the net costs for low-income students beyond the point of affordability (Advisory Committee on Student Financial Assistance, 2001; St. John, 1994). More recently, the federal courts have begun to reconsider the legality of Affirmative Action in college admission (e.g., *Hopwood v. State of Texas*) and other courts are following the precedence (e.g., *Gratz and Hamacher v. Bollinger, et al.*). College participation rates for traditional college-age African Americans have lagged behind Whites by about ten percentage points for more than a decade (U. S. Department of Education, 1998).

Unfortunately, it is unlikely that the strategies used to advocate for equal opportunity during the last half of the twentieth century will be persuasive in the new century. Instead, a new policy context requires a fundamental rethinking of both research questions and advocacy strategies. This chapter takes a step toward such a rethinking process. First, the changing policy context is examined, with an explicit focus on the role of federal and state policy in promoting equal educational opportunity and encouraging diversity. Then, we suggest a new set of foundations for guiding practical strategies for equalizing opportunity and promoting academic access for diverse groups in American society. Finally, we conclude by suggesting an agenda that can inform policymakers who are concerned about improving equity in educational opportunity.

A Changing Policy Context

During the last two decades of the twentieth century, the foundations for educational policy in the United States were systematically restructured, shifting the focus from promoting equal opportunity to promoting excellence at a lower taxpayer cost. The courts have also shifted their focus away from racial preference in college admissions and from system-wide access to a remedy for college segregation at historically Black colleges and universities (HBCUs). Given judicial trends, it is probably not reasonable to expect the courts to reverse their new positions by suddenly accepting rationales they have previously rejected. It is also unlikely that voters will elect a new Congress and President that will substantially expand resources for equalizing educational opportunity. Rather, it is crucial for advocates of diversity in higher education to build an understanding of the new policy context before rethinking their research and advocacy stra-tegies.

Desegregation at a Crossroads

Efforts to understand the new policy context appropriately start with a reexamination of policy on desegregation in education. The position of the courts on desegregation in both K-12 education and higher education changed during the 1990s, creating a new climate, disappointing those who expected judicial activism to remedy the vestiges of segregation.

The failure of federal efforts to desegregate urban schools creates a perplexing context for efforts to promote access in higher education. The federal courts have essentially declared victory by ending forced desegregation in many cities (Fossey, 1998; Orfield & Eaton, 1996). However, this is a hollow victory at best, given that America's schools were more segregated in the late 1990s than they were before the Supreme Court's 1954 decision in *Brown v. Board of Education* (Fossey, 1998; Fossey, in press). Both urban communities and urban schools are now predominantly minority. Further, since most African Americans attend urban K-12 schools, efforts to promote diversity through college admissions must contend with the fact that many African American, as well as White, students will have attended segregated schools prior to attending college.

Higher education desegregation decisions have recently focused on desegregation of public HBCUs (St. John, 1998; Williams, 1997), a development that could erode one of the traditional educational pathways for African American students. Research on HBCUs indicates that they provide a supportive environment for African American students (Allen, Epps, & Haniff, 1991; Fleming, 1984; McDonnough, Antonio, & Trent, 1997). However, the courts are now focused on providing opportunities for White students to attend HBCUs rather than for minority students to attend predominantly White institutions (Conrad, Brier, & Braxton, 1997). This could diminish some of the advantages associated with the supportive environment a predominantly Black college provides African American students. African Americans who attended segregated K-12 schools may need the opportunity to attend HBCUs for both academic and social support. Recent court decisions could shift attention away from maintaining a culture that supports African American student development (Hossler, 1997).

Thus, not only are K-12 schools more segregated, but there is the potential for a breakdown of one of the proven educational pathways for students from racially isolated K-12 schools to attend predominantly Black colleges that provide a supportive culture. This context complicates college admissions and other efforts to equalize opportunity. If segregated schools contribute to inequities in educational opportunity, then we need to ask whether there has been sufficient improvement in schools to overcome these inequities. If desegregation did not solve the problems of racial isolation and unequal opportunity in K-12 schools, then we need to ask whether the educational improvements implemented as a result of the desegregation plans and other reforms improved schools for those who suffered the most from racial isolation. Evidence from research on urban school reform suggests that reform has failed urban schools (Miron & St. John, in press), which means that the deficiencies in educational opportunity have not been resolved.

A better understanding of high school contexts is needed in college admissions, if not in efforts to support academic achievement of diverse students in colleges and universities. If HBCUs are under mandates to desegregate in order to receive funding, therefore potentially disrupting their supportive communities, and if the total opportunity to attend other four-year colleges is limited, then it is possible that children who attended racially isolated or academically inadequate urban schools will be at a competitive disadvantage for admission and success in four-year colleges.

The Decline of Affirmative Action

If it were still acceptable to use racial preferences in college admissions, then it would be easier to equalize opportunity to attend college for under-represented groups (i.e., Hispanics and African Americans). Advocates of Affirmative Action argue that the use of racial preferences can overcome some of the historic disadvantages associated with racial isolation and underfunding of urban schools. There is also some evidence to support this proposition (Bowen & Bok, 1998; Gurin, 1999). However, both the courts and the majority of voters in several states have taken an opposing position to this traditional position on Affirmative Action.

Public colleges and universities are losing the freedom to consider race explicitly in their admissions processes. In California and Washington, voters have required colleges and universities to abandon Affirmative Action. In the Texas *Hopwood* decision, the federal court ruled that the University of Texas could not give preferential treatment to African Americans and Hispanics in college admissions. Recently, the federal court also ruled that the University of Michigan's former admissions process had illegally used racial preferences (*Gratz and Hamacher v. Bollinger, et al.*). The rationale for the explicit use of racial preferences has fallen out of favor.

The origins of racial preferences in college admissions were situated in efforts to rectify injustices of segregated and inequitable educational systems. However, the rationale for ending racial preferences is rooted in the U.S. Constitution, which requires people to be treated in fair and equal ways regardless of their race or gender (Schmidt, 1998). In one sense, the position one takes on the issue of racial preferences depends on the definition of fairness one holds. As Rawls' theory of justice (1971) argues, there is a need to balance arguments about fairness for all with special consideration of those with disadvantages. Given the great disparity in K-12 schools and the consequences of racial isolation of urban schools, it is important to recognize that the vestiges of unequal education have not been removed. Fairness in admissions must be consonant with fairness of opportunities for educational preparation prior to admissions. This means that we need to find new ways to balance both types of justice considerations in this new legal context.

One possible path involves evolving new rationales for racial preference. A number of noted scholars have taken this path, including Derek Bok and Howard Bowen (1998). There is a new wave of research that indicates that integrated education and especially enrollment in courses that consider issues related to multicultural education actually contribute to intellectual development in college for all students, including majority students (Hurtado, 1999, in press). However, while this research is compelling, there is reason to question whether it will provide a sufficient rationale for continuing to use racial preferences in admissions. The argument is currently going through the federal courts in the University of Michigan undergraduate admissions case (*Gratz and Hamacher v. Bollinger, et al.*). Lower court rulings held that the University's current admissions practice was legal but its former practice (1995-1998) was illegal. The rulings are under appeal with the U.S. Sixth Circuit Court at the time of this writing.

An alternative for advocates of social justice is to consider new legal ways of constructing admissions decisions. Since the court decisions on Affirmative Action have focused explicitly on the legality of assigning points to students from underrepresented racial-ethnic groups, it should be possible to construct alternative admission criteria that ensure diversity without explicitly considering race-ethnicity as an admission criterion (Goggin, 1999). Recent simulations illustrating this can be a workable approach (see St. John, Simmons, & Musoba, 2002).

However, regardless of the path chosen, there is a need to think through the strategies for achieving diversity in college admissions in the post-Affirmative Action period. Since there are substantial inequities in educational opportunities for school children, it is possible that explicit recognition of deficiencies in the prior schools the students attended can overcome some of the vestiges of inequity in college admissions. However, admission is only part of the new problem with racial inequality.

The Decline of Federal Need-Based Grants

Federal need-based grant aid has declined substantially since 1980 (College Board, 2000; St. John, 1994;). While federal loans have expanded, the total student aid available to low-income students is inadequate (Advisory Committee on Student Financial Assistance, 2001). In 1992-93, the average college freshman from a low-income family (i.e., families earning less than $25,000) paid $4,922 in four-year public colleges after grants, loans, and other aid (Berkner & Chavez, 1997). College costs have risen faster than federal student aid since that time

(College Board, 2000), so these problems have worsened. Further, low-income students borrow substantially more than middle- and high-income students. These conditions have serious consequences for both the opportunities to attend four-year colleges and to persist to degree completion. Since more than half of the African American freshmen who attended college in 1992-93 were from families earning less than $25,000 (Berkner & Chavez, 1997), the inadequacy of federal aid contributed to the opportunity gap.

The decline in federal need-based grants has contributed directly to the widening of the opportunity gap since 1980. Using a standard of academic qualification comparable to admittance to a four-year college, an NCES report on access found that in 1994, 22.3% of college-qualified, low-income students in the freshman age group had not attended college two years after high school (Berkner & Chavez, 1997). Further, barely over half (52.5%) of the low-income high school graduates were academically qualified, indicating that many had inadequate opportunities in their K-12 education. Thus, there are both financial and academic aspects of the access problem.

The financial aspect of the access problem is not only evident in the lower college participation rate by low-income students, but also in persistence. Recent analyses of national databases indicate that low-income students are not only more likely to choose college because of low tuition and high aid than for degree or educational opportunities, but that grant aid is inadequate to promote continuous enrollment (Paulsen & St. John, 2002). Further, persistence studies using national databases not only show that low-income students are less likely to persist than middle-income students, controlling for achievement, but that debt is negatively associated with persistence (Cofer & Somers, 2000). Since low-income students usually accumulate more debt, dropping out because of inadequate finances is especially problematic. Thus, even if they can afford college enrollment initially, low-income students have substantially less financial capacity to afford continuous enrollment.

The cuts in federal grants were fueled by a new conservative ideology that maintained colleges were wasteful and that student aid was ineffectual (Bennett, 1987; Carnes, 1987; Finn, 1988; Hansen, 1983). This rationale persuaded Congress to reduce funding for federal grant programs (Cook, 1998; Parsons,

1997). However, the new policy of reducing grants and expanding loans was a primary cause of the opportunity gap. The Advisory Committee on Student Financial Assistance (2001) has recently released a report, titled *Access Denied*, that called attention to this issue, arguing that the decline in student grants has contributed to the opportunity gap.

The Apparent Failure of K-12 School Reform

Conservative criticism of the Advisory Committee's *Access Denied* (2001) report has argued that improvement in K-12 schools is needed to expand access, and if there was sufficient improvement in schools, then fewer people would need college (Finn, 2001). In the 1980s, the Reagan administration shifted the focus on federal school reform from equalizing opportunity (i.e., providing supplemental educational resources to the children most at risk) to focusing on test scores and curriculum alignment for all schools (Finn, 1990). Given that these reforms have had a nearly 20-year trial, it seems reasonable to ask whether they have contributed to an expansion in opportunity. If they have not, then such reforms are not the answer to reducing the opportunity gap.

One indicator of the efficacy of school reforms is whether they have improved the percentage of students who graduate from high school. Since the mid 1970s, high school graduation rates have actually declined slightly (U. S. Department of Education, 2001), indicating that educational opportunity has not increased as a result of these reforms. One recent study examined the impact of implementing a high stakes graduation test in Indiana (Manset & Washburn, in press), finding that special education students and urban schools were negatively impacted by the new tests because fewer of these students graduated. This study illustrates an underlying problem with test-driven reform ideology. By introducing more tests into the system and forcing an alignment of curriculum with tests, educational systems can force students out who need special assistance and force more students into special education.

The latest wave of federal education reform has emphasized using "research based" methods. Both the *Reading Excellence Act* and the *Comprehensive School Reform Demonstration Act* provide funding for schools to adopt reforms that have a proven research base. Initial studies on these reforms indicate that some reform models actually do reduce special education referral and grade retention in elementary schools (St. John, Manset, Chung, Musoba, et al., in press; St. John, Manset, Chung, Simmons, in press). Thus, there is an obvious need for more research on the effects of these reforms. It is also apparent that providing schools the opportunity to adopt reform models that have a research base could be a viable approach for keeping more children in the educational system and for increasing the percentage of students who are prepared for college.

Clearly, K-12 school reform must be part of the solution to the access problem through enhancing academic preparation. However, it is crucial to recognize that past reforms have contributed to the problem. While the newest wave of research-based reforms provides reasonable hope, substantial gains must be made just to regain the equity level that has been lost.

Breakdown in Education Policy

The current education policy context has many impediments to equal opportunity in both K-12 education and higher education. While the test-driven reforms overtly promote opportunity for all, they speed the decline in equity. The cuts in federal student grants may be the primary cause of the new inequality in opportunity, but failed efforts at K-12 reform have also contributed to the problem.

In this context, the shifting focus of higher education desegregation to desegregating HBCUs from desegregating Predominately White Institutions (PWIs) and the decline in Affirmative Action limit the mechanisms that can be used to remedy the problem. Historically colleges used racial preferences to ensure diversity in college admissions, but their ability to follow this path has been curtailed, if not extinguished. Unfortunately, the notion that equal educational opportunity should be an outcome of college desegregation is no longer the focus of federal desegregation litigation in the post-*Fordice* environment (St. John, 1998; Williams, 1988). We clearly need to take a fresh look at the challenge of promoting equal opportunity.

Rethinking Advocacy

Current conditions surrounding academic access and opportunity necessitate a rethinking of policy strategies by those who are committed to promoting equal educational opportunity. Before considering alternative strategies, however, we should revisit the theory of social justice, as a foundation for rethinking policy strategies.

Refocusing on Social Justice

Rawls (1971) identified two principles of justice. The first, "each person is to have an equal right to the most extensive total system of equal basic liberties compatible with a similar system of liberty for all" (p. 302), and the second, "social and economic inequalities are to be arranged so that they are both: (a) to the greatest benefit to the least advantaged, consistent with the just savings principle, and (b) attached to offices and positions of fair equality of opportunity" (p. 302). The first principle clearly argued for equal treatment, a rationale related to arguments for eliminating racial preferences in admissions. However, before we leap to the conclusion that it should be applied to the current access problem, we need to consider Rawls's first priority rule for applying the principles:

> The principles of justice are ranked in lexical order and therefore liberty can be restricted only for the sake of liberty. There are two cases: (a) a less extensive liberty must strengthen the total system of liberty shared by all; (b) a less than equal liberty must be acceptable to those with lesser liberty. (p. 302)

Whether individuals argue for affirmative methods of intervention depends on the way they view the evidence relative to "fair and equal opportunity." In higher education there was fair and equal opportunity in the late 1970s (1976-78), at least as measured by the near equal participation rates. As the previous review indicates, policies have shifted in ways during the intervening twenty years that have increased inequities. We think it is too early to eliminate the emphasis on racial preference and equal opportunity (e.g., St. John & Hossler, 1998; St. John, Simmons, & Musoba, 2002). However, we also recognize it may no longer be possible to rest policy arguments on this principle alone.

The new legal environment clearly argues that Rawls's first principle rather than the second should be applied in college admissions. Federal desegregation strategies now promote desegregation of historically Black colleges more ardently than they promote desegregation of predominantly White colleges. The decline of Affirmative Action further illustrates there has been a shift in emphasis and logic used to litigate and orchestrate. The new challenge for advocates of social justice in educational policy is to promote access in ways that are compatible with the equal treatment principle, especially with respect to the elimination of racial preference, yet help remedy the inequality in economic opportunity that has emerged.

Financial Access

Since financial access has surfaced as a problem in higher education, it is important to start with a workable definition of financial access. We have defined financial access as: "the ability to afford continuous enrollment in the lowest cost two-year and four-year program available to applicants, given their ability and prior performance" (St. John, Musoba, & Simmons, 2001, p. 2). This definition of financial access is consistent with the first principle of justice, with respect to racial preference, but also provides a basis for constructing and assessing policy aimed at promoting equal opportunity across racial and economic groups. The erosion of federal student aid programs has limited the ability of states to ensure financial access for their citizens. The unmet need for the average low-income student in public college with average costs is currently too high to maintain continuous enrollment unless there is supplemental grant support from states and/or institutions.

A recent analysis of the 21st Century Scholars Program in Indiana illustrates that the financial access problem can be resolved by states, but it takes a substantial financial commitment to need-based student grants (St. John, Musoba, & Simmons, 2001). This program asked low-income eighth graders (i.e., those eligible for free or reduced lunch) to make commitments to prepare for college academically and to remain alcohol and drug-free. In 1997-98 the average freshman in the program received a state grant of over three thousand dollars, an amount nearly equal to the average unmet need after Pell grants, the largest federal need-based grant. Our analyses of within-year persistence by freshmen revealed that recipients of 21st Century grants were more likely to persist than were unaided students and that low-income students had the same probability of persisting as other students (St. John, Musoba, & Simmons, 2001). Further, a series of studies of within-year persistence by college students in Indiana in the 1990s, a period when federal grants declined and Indiana grants climbed, indicated financial aid remained adequate to equalize the opportunity to persist (Hu & St. John, 2001; St. John, Hu, & Weber, 2000, 2001). Thus, the 21st Century Scholars Program in Indiana was an integral part of a state finance strategy that has ensured financial access.

The solution to the financial access problem relates directly to the adequacy of state student financial aid, given the inadequacy of federal student aid and the ongoing conservative call to reduce federal taxes. Thus, advocates of equal educational opportunity must promote adequate funding of need-based state grant programs. Promoting greater cooperation between states and the federal government on a second-tier grant strategy might also be a viable approach. However, it is unlikely that the federal government will reinvest in federal grants at a level approximating the investment made in the 1970s.

Academic Access

Our definition of financial access leaves colleges and universities in control of academic access, whether students are qualified for initial and continued enrollment. The admitting institution retains responsibility for determining academic access while the K-12 education system and the student are responsible for adequate academic preparation. This definition of academic access is not only consistent with the notions of academic qualification used by the National Center for Education Statistics (e.g., Berkner & Chavez, 1997), but also provides a basis for rethinking strategies that promote financial access. We explicitly consider admissions policy, postsecondary encouragement, and school reform.

Admissions Policy. While states may set general policies for admission standards and admission practices, the process of admitting and educating students remains an institutional responsibility. In reaction to the post-Affirmative Action litigation, some states have emphasized high school grade point averages instead of test scores as part of the criteria used in admissions. This approach implicitly adjusts for inequities in high schools, consistent with the assumption that students should not be penalized for attending low-quality high schools. This assumption is compatible with the second principle of justice, but does not use racial-ethnic preferences as a basis for promoting equity. If we hold to this assumption, then there are at least four possible approaches to promoting equal opportunity in academic admission processes in public universities:

- Using grade point averages, an approach recommended by Olivas (1997, 1999) and used in Texas, Florida, and California, states that have adjusted to the post-Affirmative Action environment.
- Adjusting test scores using a merit index constructed from the high school average, an approach proposed by Goggin (1999) and empirically tested by St. John, Simmons, & Musoba (2002).
- Creating an empirical index for high school quality in a state, based on high school achievement test scores and other indicators, an approach that is conceptually consistent with Goggin's merit aware approach and potentially more equitable than adjusting test scores.
- Adjusting applications for SES indicators, a class based affirmative action advocated by Kahlenberg (1996), and tested with mixed results (Bernal, Cabrera, & Terenzini, 2000).

Of the possible approaches, we think the methods that index for academic inequities among high schools (i.e., SAT or high school achievement tests) hold the greatest potential because they hold children harmless for high school effects without inducing grade inflation. Using GPA as a primary criterion for admissions can encourage grade inflation in high schools. However, adjusting standardized tests avoids this problem, while encouraging equity in admissions decisions and encouraging more students to take admissions tests. However, there is a need for more research on all possible methods, as a means of testing how well they work in practice. Recently we collaborated on a study that estimated effects of the SAT and the merit index on persistence (St. John, Hu, Simmons, & Musoba, 2001). We found that the merit index, an adjustment of the SAT for the high school average, predicted persistence as well as the SAT. We think that further experimentation and testing of different approaches to adapting admission standards is appropriate and needed.

The challenge of providing fair and just admissions practices will likely become more acute in the future given the relative erosion of opportunity for African Americans and Hispanics to attend public four-year colleges. Between 1990 and 1996 the number of full time equivalent (FTE) students enrolled in public four-year colleges actually declined while the number in public two-year colleges and private four-year colleges increased (U.S. Department of Education, 1998). This erosion in opportunity was attributable to a new set of financial circumstances, including rising tuition and reduced grant aid. States have reduced spending on public four-year colleges, which has influenced tuition to rise. Higher costs of attending and lower student aid have contributed to the financial access problem (Advisory Committee on Student Financial Aid, 2001).

Further, given the need to expand access in the next few decades, it is possible that states will expand two-year systems rather than four-year systems (Council for Aid to Education, 1997; National Center for Public Policy and Higher Education, 2000). If this happens, then there will be more competition for limited opportunity to attend four-year colleges. Thus, it is crucial to evolve fair and just approaches to admissions that maintain academic access for diverse groups.

Academic Support: Once students are admitted, a tacit contract is formed between a college and a student. Essentially the student is agreeing to work at a level sufficient to maintain enrollment while colleges are agreeing that the student has the capability to maintain enrollment, provided the institution offers sufficient academic opportunity and support. We think that when colleges admit students who are at risk of failure without providing adequate support opportunities, they are contributing to a "revolving door" (Cope & Hannah, 1975), rather than fulfilling the commitment they make at admission, even open admission. This standard is infrequently discussed in academic meetings, but should be a central concern for both admissions officers and academic administrators, as well as for the assess-ment of academic programs.

The persistence studies of college students enrolled in pub-lic higher education in Indiana reveal that achieving below C grades is a major predictor of dropout (St. John, Hu, & Weber, 2000, in press), especially for minority students (Hu & St. John, 2001) and freshmen (St. John, Musoba, & Simmons, 2001). These studies reveal that even when financial access is guaran-teed by states, that academic access, especially the ability to remain academically qualified for continuous enrollment, re-mains a challenge for public colleges and universities, at least in Indiana.

Postsecondary Encouragement: A new federal program – Gaining Early Awareness and Readiness for Undergraduate Programs (GEAR UP) – funds organizations that provide en-couragement to students to attend college. The theory behind this approach to promoting access is that students will be more likely to prepare for college if they are aware of the opportuni-ties available and of financial resources available to them. There is substantial evidence that postsecondary encouragement can improve college participation rates if there is adequate stu-dent aid (Hossler & Schmit, 1995).

However, as long as substantial numbers of academically qualified and highly motivated students do not attend college, a situation that obviously exists at the present time (Berkner & Chavez, 1997), there is little reason to assume expanding en-couragement will make a difference for students from low-in-come families. In spite of this limitation, there is reason to ex-pect that providing early encouragement to students in middle school and high school can promote better preparation (Hossler, Schmit, & Vesper, 1998), if the schools have adequate course offerings.

School Reform: School reform potentially provides the fourth component of a coherent strategy aimed at expanding academic access and equalizing the opportunity to attend col-lege. However, it is crucial that K-12 education shift away from tightening tests and curriculum in ways that force more children out of the mainstream. The alternative is to engage schools in reform processes that enable more children to maintain aca-demic progress at a sufficient level to stay in the educational mainstream. Toward this end, we think that researchers need to assess whether reforms actually reduce failure (i.e., retention and special education referral) and improve the percentage of children who complete high school and who are prepared for college.

An Agenda: Research Informing Policy

We can now propose an agenda for researchers and reformers who are concerned about improving equity in educational attainment. A central feature of this strategy involves treating opportunity-related outcomes as goals of education, goals that merit attention along with more frequently measured achievement related outcomes. We think that opportunity and achievement should be put back into balance in education policy. Specifically, we recommend that:

- K-12 school reform should be evaluated based on whether it improves the percentage of children achieving on or above grade level (i.e., reducing dropout, grade retention, and referral to special education) and high school graduation rates, along with achievement test scores and pass rates.
- Financial access should be evaluated based on whether economically diverse students who are academically qualified have equal opportunity to enroll, as well as by whether low-income and minority students have equal probabilities of persisting, controlling for academic achievement.
- Academic preparation should be evaluated based on how well high schools prepare students for college, as measured by percentages of students, by income level, completing a college preparatory curriculum and standardized-test scores and pass rates.
- Academic access should be evaluated by percentage of academically prepared students, by income group, who attend college. This is a minimum standard. Ideally students with college preparatory coursework would go to four-year colleges.

In addition, equal opportunity can be given more explicit consideration if researchers and policymakers consider how these outcomes vary for economically and ethnically diverse groups in state educational systems. This research-based approach provides a workable alternative to the current direction of education policy, which does not give adequate consideration to equity issues.

It is crucial that we reconsider measures of equal opportunity along with the traditional measures of educational achievement that are now used to evaluate education policy in the U.S. Educational policy is overly focused on the academic outcomes without adequately considering opportunity-related outcomes. Thus, a more balanced approach is needed in education policy in states and at the federal level.

Notes

1. This approach is potentially more equitable because states have relatively complete information on high schools and only a limited percentage of students from high schools actually take the SAT test.

References

Advisory Committee on Student Financial Assistance. (2001). *Access denied.* Washington, DC: Authors.

Allen, W. A., Epps, E. G., & Haniff, N. Z. (Eds.) (1991). *College in Black and White: African American students in predominantly White and in historically Black public universities.* Albany, NY: State University of New York Press.

Bennett, W. J. (1987). Our greedy colleges. *New York Times,* 18 February, I 31.

Berkner, L., & Chavez, L. (1997). *Access to postsecondary education for the 1992 high school graduates.* Washington, DC: U.S. Dept. of Education, Office of Educational Research and Improvement.

Bernal, E. M., Cabrera, A. F., & Terenzini, P. T. (2000). The relationship between race and socioeconomic status (SES): Implications for institutional research and admissions policies. *Removing Vestiges,* (1), 6-13.

Bowen, W. G., & Bok, D. (1998). *The shape of the river: Long-term consequences of considering race in college and university admissions.* Princeton, NJ: Princeton University Press.

Brown, M. C., & Hendrickson, R. M. (1997). Public historically Black colleges at the crossroads: *United States v. Fordice* and higher education desegregation. *Journal for a Just and Caring Education, 3* (1), 95-113.

Carnes, B. M. (1987). The campus cost explosion: College tuitions are unnecessarily high. *Policy Review, 40,* 68-71.

Cofer, J., & Somers, P. (2000). A comparison of the influence of debtload on the persistence of students at public and private colleges. *Journal of Student Financial Aid 30* (2), 39-58.

College Board. (2000). *Trends in student aid.* Washington, D.C.: College Board.

Conrad, C. F., Brier, E. M., & Braxton, J. M. (1997). Factors contributing to the matriculation of White students in public HBCUs. *Journal for a Just and Caring Education, 3* (1), 37-62.

Cook, C. (1998). *Lobbying for higher education: How colleges and universities influence federal policy.* Nashville, TN: Vanderbilt University Press.

Cope, R., & Hannah, W. (1975). *Revolving college doors: The causes and consequences of dropping out, stopping out, and transferring.* New York: Wiley.

Council for Aid to Education. (1997). *Breaking the social contract: The fiscal crisis in higher education.* Santa Monica, CA: RAND.

Finn, C. E., Jr. (1988, July/August). Judgment time for higher education: In the court of public opinion. *Change,* 35-38.

Finn, C. E., Jr. (1990). The biggest reform of all. *Phi-Delta-Kappan, 71* (8), 584-92.

Finn, C. E., Jr. (2001, February 21). College isn't for everyone. *USA Today,* p. 14A.

Fleming, J. (1984). *Blacks in college.* San Francisco: Jossey-Bass Publishers.

Fossey, R. E. (1998). Desegregation is not enough: Facing the truth about urban schools. In R. E. Fossey (ed.), *Readings on equal education, Vol. 15, Race, the courts, and equal education: The limits of the law.* New York: AMS Press.

Fossey, R. E. (in press). Desegregation is over in the inner cities: What do we do now? In L. Miron & E. P. St. John (eds.),

Reinterpreting urban school reform. Albany, NY: State University of New York Press.

Gladieux, L. E., & Wolanin, T. (1976). *Congress and the colleges: The national politics of higher education.* Lexington, MA: Lexington Books.

Goggin, W. J. (1999, May). A "merit-aware" model for college admissions and affirmative action. *Postsecondary Education Opportunity Newsletter,* (Published by Tom Mortenson), 6-12.

Gurin, P. (1999). Expert report of Patricia Gurin. In *The compelling need for diversity in higher education* [On line.] Available at http://www.umich.edu/~urel/admissions/legal/expert/gurintoc.html.

Hansen, W. L. (1983). The impact of student financial aid on access. In J. Froomkin (ed.), *The crisis in higher education.* New York: Academy of Political Science.

Hossler, D. (1997). Scholarly research and personal reflections. *Just and Caring Education, 3* (1), 114-126.

Hossler, D. & Schmit, J. (1995). Postsecondary encouragement programs: The Indiana experiment. In E. P. St John (ed.), *Rethinking tuition and student aid strategies.* New Directions in Higher Education, No. 89, 27-40. San Francisco: Jossey-Bass.

Hossler, D., Schmit, J., & Vesper, N. (1998). *Going to college: How social, economic, and educational factors influence the decisions students make.* Baltimore: Johns Hopkins University Press.

Hu, S., & St. John, E. P. (2001). Student persistence in a public higher education system: Understanding racial/ethnic differences. *Journal of Higher Education, 72* (3), 265-286.

Hurtado, S. (1999). Reaffirming educators' judgment: Educational value of diversity, *Journal of Liberal Education,* Spring, 24-31. Washington, DC: American Association of Colleges and Universities.

Hurtado, S. (in press). Linking diversity with educational purpose: College outcomes associated with diversity in the faculty and student body. In G. Orfield and C. Edley (eds.), Harvard Civil Rights Project.

Kahlenberg, R. D. (1996). *The remedy: Class, race and affirmative action.* New York: Basic Books.

Manset, G. & Washburn, S. (in press) Inclusive education in high stakes, high poverty environments: The case of students with learning disabilities in Indiana's urban schools and the Graduation Qualifying Exam. In L. F. Miron & E. P. St. John (eds.), *Reinterpreting urban school reforms: A critical-empirical review.* NY: SUNY Press.

McDonnough, P. M., Antonio, A. L., & Trent, J. W. (1997). Black students, Black colleges: An African American college choice model. *Journal for a Just and Caring Education* 3 (1), 9-36.

Miron, L. F. & St. John, E. P., (eds.) (in press) *Reinterpreting urban school reform: A critical-empirical review.* Albany, NY: SUNY Press.

National Center for Public Policy and Higher Education. (2000). *Measuring up 2000.* Washington, DC: Authors.

Olivas, M.A. (1997). Constitutional criteria: The social science and common law of admissions decisions in higher education. *University of Colorado Law Review, 68* (4), 1065-1121.

Olivas, M. A. (1999). Higher education admissions and the search for one important thing. *University of Arkansas at Little Rock Law Review, 21,* 993-1024.

Orfield, G., & Eaton, S. E. (1996). *Dismantling desegregation: The quiet reversal of Brown v. Board of Education.* New York: Free Press.

Parsons, M. D. (1997). *Power and politics: Federal higher education policymaking in the 1990s.* Albany, NY: State University of New York Press.

Paulsen, M. B., & St. John, E. P. (2002). Social class and college costs: Examining the financial nexus between college choice and persistence. *Journal of Higher Education, 73,* 189-236.

Rawls, J. (1971). *A theory of justice.* Cambridge, MA: Belknap Press of Harvard University Press.

St. John, E. P. (1994). *Prices, productivity and investment: Assessing financial strategies in higher education.* ASHE/ERIC Higher Education Report, No. 3. Washington, D. C.: George Washington University.

St. John, E. P. (1998). Higher education desegregation in the post-Fordice legal environment: An historical perspective. In R. E. Fossey (ed.), *Readings on equal education, Vol. 15, Race, the courts, and equal education: The limits of the law* (pp. 101-122). New York: AMS Press.

St. John, E. P., & Hossler, D. (1998). Higher education desegregation in the post-*Fordice* legal environment: A critical-empirical perspective. In R. E. Fossey, (ed.), *Readings on equal education, Vol. 15, Race, the courts, and equal education: The limits of the law* (pp.123-156). New York: AMS Press.

St. John, E. P., Hu, S., Simmons, A., & Musoba, G. D. (2001). Aptitude versus merit: What matters in persistence. *Review of Higher Education, 24,* 131-152.

St. John, E. P., Hu, S., & Weber, J. (2000). Keeping public colleges affordable: A study of persistence in Indiana's public colleges and universities. *Journal of Student Financial Aid, 29* (2), 21-32.

St. John, E. P., Hu, S., & Weber, J. (2001). State policy and the affordability of public higher education: The influence of state grants on persistence in Indiana. *Research in Higher Education, 42,* 401-428.

St. John, E. P., Manset, G., Chung, C. G., Musoba, G. D., Loescher, S., Simmons, A. B., Gordon, D., & Hossler, C. A. (in press). Comprehensive school reform: An exploratory study. In L. F. Miron & E. P. St. John (eds.), *Reinterpreting urban school reform: A critical-empirical review.* Albany, NY: State University of New York Press.

St. John, E. P., Manset, G., Chung, C. G., Simmons, A. B., Musoba, G. D., Manoil, K., & Worthington, K. (in press). Research-based reading reform: The impact of state-funded interventions on educational outcomes in urban schools. In L. F. Miron & E. P. St. John (eds.), *Reinterpreting urban school reform: A critical-empirical review.* Albany, NY: State University of New York Press.

St. John, E. P., Musoba, G. D., & Simmons, A. B. (2001). *Keeping the promise: The impact of Indiana's 21st century scholars program.* Paper presented at the 18th Annual Student Financial Aid Research Network Conference: A Joint NASSGAP/NCHELP Project.

St. John, E. P., Simmons, A., & Musoba, G. D. (2001). Merit-aware admissions in public universities: Increasing diversity. *Thought and Action, 27* (2), 35-46.

Schmidt, P. (1998, October 30). U. of Michigan prepares to defend admissions policy in court. *Chronicle of Higher Education,* p. A32.

U.S. Department of Education, National Center for Education Statistics. (1998). *The condition of education 1998.* Washington, D.C.: U.S. Government Printing Office.

U.S. Department of Education, National Center for Education Statistics. (2001). *Digest of Education Statistics,* 2000. NCES 2001-034. By Thomas D. Snyder. Project Dir., Charlene M. Hoffman. Prod. Mgr. Washington, DC: NCES. [On-line] Available at: http://nces.ed.gov/pubs2001/digest/

U.S. Department of Education (1997). Comprehensive School Reform Act. Public Law 105-78. Appropriations Act. Conference Report: House Report No. 105-309. [On-line] Available at: http://www.ed.gov/offices/OESE/compreform.

U.S. Department of Education (1999). Title VIII – Reading Excellence Act. An amendment to the Elementary and Secondary Education Act. [On-line] Available at: http://www.ed.gov/offices/OESE/REA/

Williams, J. B. (1988). Title VI regulation of higher education. In J. B. Williams (ed.), *Desegregating America's colleges and universities: Title VI regulation of higher education* (pp. 33-53). New York: Teachers College Press.

Williams, J. B. (1997). *Race discrimination in higher education.* New York: Praeger.

Wong, K. K. (in press). Federal Title I as a reform strategy in urban schools. In L. F. Miron & E. P. St. John (eds.), *Reinterpreting urban school reform: A critical-empirical review.* Albany, NY: SUNY Press.

Table of Legal Cases

Regents of Univ. of California. v. Bakke, 438 U.S. 265, 287, 98 S. Ct. 2733, 2746, 57 L. Ed. 2d 750 (1978)

Brown v. The Board of Education of Topeka, Kansas, 349 U.S. 294 (1955).

Gratz and Hamacher v. Bollinger, et al., No. 97-75231.

Hopwood v. State of Texas, 78 F.3d 932 (5th Cir. 1996) cert. Denied, 116 S. Ct. 2581 (1996).

United States v. Fordice, 505 U.S. 717 (1992).

SECTION III.

Conclusion

CHAPTER 10

THE IMPACT OF ACCESS AND EQUITY IN HIGHER EDUCATION: THE ENDURING MEANING OF EDUCATIONAL OPPORTUNITY

Pamela S. Angelle & Elizabeth A. Kemper

This volume of *Readings on Equal Education* offers a lens through which to view the current state of higher education in terms of providing equity and access to students. Through examinations of demographic data, empirical evidence, and research studies, the authors in this volume focus on facets of higher education which have been advantageous to, and those which have been deleterious to women, students of color, and students who fall under the umbrella of ADA. In this concluding chapter, we scrutinize those components of equal opportunity presented and draw conclusions and recommendations for policy and practice. In doing so, we find that the waters of higher education policy, with regard to the groups we examine, are indeed murky.

In the introduction to this volume, Brown considers whether pursuit of universal access requires unequal treatment. While answering in the affirmative, he takes care to distinguish the difference between equity and equality. Equity, in contrast to equality, "requires that the distribution of social resources be sufficient to the condition that is being treated (Gordon, 1995, in Brown, this volume). In the interest of discerning between equity and equality, this volume examines the vast array of different types of students who sees access to higher education, along with the challenges and opportunities afforded to him/her.

The Collegiate Context

The stereotype of the student who seeks access to American higher education has expanded over the past twenty years to include greater numbers of women, students of color, and non-traditional age adults. With this expanded picture, institutions face the task of addressing the social, political, and financial issues inherent in attempts to diversify. Lanaan and Brown (chapter 1), as well as Aragon and Zamani (chapter 2) and Richardson (chapter 3), note that community colleges and distance education offer alternatives to underrepresented groups,. As a result, mainstream institutions have had to step back and reexamine their policies with respect to increasing admissions for diverse student populations. As these institutions ponder their role and their policies as they relate to women and students of color, minority serving institutions and community colleges have defined their missions in light of the students they serve and have offered culturally based initiatives. As a result, these same institutions have watched enrollments increase (see Aragon and Zamani, chapter 2). Unfortunately, lack of sufficient state and federal funding has hampered efforts to address the instructional needs of minority students.

Distance education offers another alternative to traditional education and a propitious means by which to reach a greater number of students. However, the instrument of instructional delivery, the computer, is often not accessible to minority students and students of poverty. Richardson (chapter 3) argues that possession of cultural goods (in this case, computers) equates to power (in this case, education). Thus, students who lack access to computers (here, students of color and/or poverty) are not privy to the opportunities afforded from distance education. This lack of opportunity translates to a failure to provide access to higher education and a continued domination of the Eurocentric culture. Unfortunately, attempts to move the barriers of the digital divide generally have not met with success.

At first glance, federal legislation and university policy might be seen as the keys with which to open the doors of equity and access for students and faculty alike. However, vague court rulings and the instability of policy, shifting with the winds of political philosophy, cause difficulty when attempts are made to unlock the doors. University policy and practice regarding the recruitment of minority faculty has been implemented; however, retention and promotion of that same faculty has not been as successful (see Tillman, chapter 5). Just as communication and education regarding minority faculty is important, so is education regarding the compliance demands of ADA, not only for university personnel but for those students with disabilities as well, as noted by Richards (chapter 4). In this case, diversity is not limited to race, class, or gender but is a challenge where an awareness of the rights of all students with learning disabilities is desired and necessary.

The Policy Context

Part II of the volume delves more deeply into those legal and policy issues which both challenge and frustrate the higher education community. Disparities in the financing of higher education (see Alexander, chapter 6) directly impact the ability of students to pay tuition and obtain financial aid. Federal policy has failed to insure that states adequately invest in higher education, thus, limiting access to universities for many students. While race conscious programs, such as the Banneker Scholars Program, as examined by Trent and Eatman (chapter 8), may positively impact students of color, the courts have failed to draw a clear line for colleges and universities amid attempts to diversify their student population. As Otto so aptly notes (chapter 6), "the unsettled nature of this legal question [whether to award scholarships based on race] makes it very difficult for public colleges and universities to be confident that the diversity and affirmative action policies that they fashion with the best of intentions will withstand the toughest legal scrutiny" (p. 125).

Title VI of the Civil Rights Act of 1964 requires universities to take affirmative action on behalf of those groups which have experienced discrimination. Many universities that have attempted to use race as part of their admissions policy, however, have found themselves embroiled in legal battles. As Otto points out, the courts have not been kind to higher education attempts to attain a diverse student population through affirmative action or scholarship programs. While using racial preferences in admissions has "fallen out of favor" with the courts, racial preferences were originally set in policy as a way to "rectify injustices of segregated and inequitable educational systems" (St. John & Musoba, chapter 9, p. 175). Left to walk a precarious tightrope, with the Fourteenth Amendment and Title VI on one side and rulings in *Regents of the University of California v. Bakke, Podberesky v. Kirwan,* and *Hopwood v. State of Texas* on the other, universities struggle to keep their balance.

The final chapter in Part II of this volume addresses that balance (St. John & Musoba, chapter 9). As the new century begins, federal policy has shifted to outcome-based educational standards, rather than focus on ensuring equity. As a result, higher education policy makers must also shift their stance on methods by which to equalize opportunities for all students. Seeking this equalization of opportunities to embrace higher education, we find that the U.S. Constitution poses a conundrum. The Fourteenth Amendment of the Constitution as well as Title VI of the Civil Rights Act of 1964 call for diversity of student populations and the opportunity for all students to attend institutions of higher learning. However, turning to the courts for guidance, universities have received mixed messages.

Holding that the test for constitutionality lay with "strict scrutiny" analysis, that is, whether the policy serves a "compelling governmental interest" and whether the policy is "narrowly tailored" to achieve that interest (Otto, chapter 6), higher education is left with no accurate compass for guidance. The difficulty rests in the ability to prove that past discrimination by the university existed and that there was a need to limit scholarships to one race; instead, the courts noted that discrimination is a societal issue (United States. Fourth District Court of Appeals. *Podberesky v. Kirwan.* 38 F.3d 147 1994). Likewise, the Fifth Circuit noted that

> Even if the law school's alleged current lingering reputation in the minority community – and the perception that the school is a hostile environment for minorities – were considered to be the present effects of past discrimination, rather than the result of societal discrimination, they could not constitute compelling interests justifying the use of racial classifications in admissions (*Hopwood v. Texas*, 78 F.3d 932, 953 (5th Cir. 1996)).

In addition, the courts determined that the university goal of achieving a racially diverse student body was not sufficient to be considered a compelling interest (*Hopwood v. Texas*, 78 F.3d 932, 953 [5th Cir.1996]).

Moreover, the financial burden of higher education is an additional obstacle to the pursuit of a college education for minority students. As educational costs have risen, federal student aid has declined. Student loans are insufficient for many students of color as the cost of books, living, and transportation increase at a far too rapid rate. Thus, if minority students are able to jump the hurdle of admission to college, the cost of education trips them at the next hurdle.

Emerging Themes from This Volume: Recommendations for Policy and Practice

The ideas presented in this volume represent a variety of viewpoints across the higher education arena. Three main strands of commonality emerge from these diverse writings. They are: the need for higher education to accommodate and value all types of diversity; the need for stronger kindergarten through college connections to enhance the ability of students from any background to have equitable access to higher education; and, the need for coherent and noncontradictory guidance to link policy and practice across all fifty states.

Diversity
Higher education must better acknowledge the need and value of accommodating students with all types of diversity, from ethnicity to disabilities. As several authors in this volume strongly illustrated, there is a powerful need for policy makers in higher education to recognize the reality of valuing and accommodating the many diversities students bring to the higher education setting. The "typical" college student is no longer very typical, and the processes and procedures developed within the higher education community must change to better meet the needs of *all* students.

Universities must approach this public recognition of a more diverse student body with caution, however. While Aragon and Zamani (chapter 2) applaud the efforts of minority serving and women's institutions in reaching those students often overlooked by predominantly white institutions, diversity does not result from these efforts. Likewise, the uniqueness of community colleges to serve student groups who may be marginalized often ensures access but does not insure diversity.

As so aptly pointed out by Richardson (chapter 3), offering distance education courses in efforts to reach greater numbers of students has resulted in a conspicuous absence of diversity. As universities target efforts at outreach, assumptions cannot be made regarding basic skill levels and technological hardware. Evaluations of distance education courses in light of the assumptions are called for.

Evaluation and monitoring of higher education institutions should also include an examination of compliance with ADA. Richards (chapter 4) recommends ongoing faculty and staff professional development regarding the rights of students with disabilities. Providing services to the needs of this diverse student population extends beyond facilities. Services to students must include programs, policies, and accommodations as well.

Connecting the Path from Kindergarten to College

There appears to be a vast sense of disconnection linking a student's public school life from kindergarten to a state college or university. As a group, minority students often attend K-12 public schools with the least qualified teachers, fewest resources, and less overall funding. These impediments make creating a competitive application to a major university more difficult, even before factoring such family and social barriers as being the first in the family to go on to higher education. Such barriers usually keep minority students from having the competitive edge necessary to gain admission to a selective institution, thus, limiting their choices in postsecondary education to regional or community colleges.

As pointed out by Alexander (chapter 6), great disparity exists in the individual states as far as tax effort and funding for higher education is concerned. There is great irony in the fact that wealthy states tend to target private higher education institutions, while those states who can least afford to, tend to offer a greater tax effort towards public higher education. Obviously, the discrepancy in tax effort limits access for students of poverty.

Alexander calls for a federal policy to eliminate these state to state disparities. Economic incentives for greater investment in higher education can ensure not only equal opportunity but higher levels of access. Federal incentives may allow states then to concentrate on improving the resources in K-12 schools, thus providing a sound educational base for those students who choose to continue on to higher education.

Creating Coherent Legislation

The most biting theme which emerges from this volume is the lack of uniformity in the legislation which governs affirmative action practice and the continued inaction of the U.S. Supreme Court to address this topic. It is absurd that in the twenty-first century affirmative action policy across the United States is interpreted differently, depending upon the circuit court region within which one resides. The unwillingness of the U.S. Supreme Court to hear cases regarding affirmative action speaks to the complexity with which the issue is imbued, but does not excuse their inaction on the subject.

While education has been interpreted as a state-based forum, the federal government has, nonetheless, placed demands upon state educational institutions to conform to guidelines. On the one hand, federal legislation in the form of Title VI has required affirmative action in higher education policy regarding admissions and scholarship funding. However, when attempts are made to implement this policy the Supreme Court has either refused to grant *certiorari* or the Circuit Courts have struck down the policies. Thus, higher education is left with the dilemma of attempting to follow a law while receiving no guidance from the federal level on how the law should be correctly followed.

Universities have walked a fine line between affirmative action and reverse discrimination. As Otto (chapter 7) points out, when higher education policy regarding diversity is made, then implemented, the expectation is that the policy will be challenged in the courts. While a diverse student body should be the goal of every institution of higher learning, the Supreme Court pointed out that race should be only one of many factors in making admissions decisions to achieve this diversity. Thus, equal opportunity is again offered, but with little progress made in the way of access and equity.

Conclusion

The concepts of access and equity in higher education are quite complex. An easy resolution to their inherent conflict does not appear to be on the horizon. Striving for access and equity in higher education is a conflict that is intertwined with the history of the United States, making more difficult the ability to separate personal feelings from personal struggle. Attempts to gain power over who has access and what is equitable will exist as long as policy conditions continue to support enclaves of privilege, exclusivity, and superiority.

The three themes which pull from the various strands throughout this volume, the need to accept and embrace diversity, the need to make connections from kindergarten through college, and the need for clear, cogent, and coherent policy guidelines for affirmative action, must be acknowledged by those that create and implement higher education policy before real change in the realm of higher education can occur. To accomplish true access and equity within higher education requires a reconceptualization of the purposes and goals of higher education as well as reallocation of funding in order to support that effort. Higher education has made great strides in affording equal opportunity to the diverse student population of the United States. However, a clear path to access and equity in higher education remains elusive.

Table of Legal Cases

Hopwood v. State of Texas, 78 F.3d 932 (5th Cir. 1996), *cert. denied*, 518 U.S. 1033 (1996).

Podberesky v. Kirwan, 38 F.3d 147 (4th Cir. 1994), *cert. denied*, 514 U.S. 1128 (1995).